THREAD PAINTING

Liz Hubbard

Thread Painting

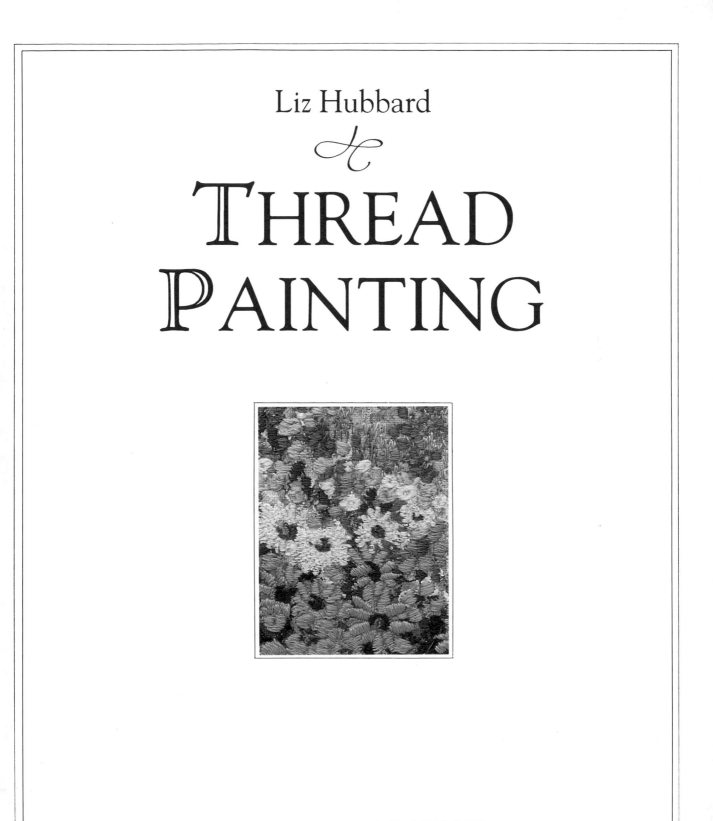

A DAVID & CHARLES CRAFT BOOK

Contents

(page 2) 'St Clement's Cottages'

For my mother

'Broom Hill Wood'

INTRODUCTION

Thread Painting is a newly developed art form in which the unusual combination of familiar materials and equipment brings about an exciting and novel way of making pictures. It is not a style of painting. All you need to begin is a domestic electric sewing-machine which has a swing needle facility, some fabric, paints and normal sewing threads.

Anyone who enjoys colour, light and shade, drawing and texture, or who has an interest in the craft of painting or embroidery, should find Thread Painting a stimulating medium with which to experiment. The results are particularly attractive, having outstanding qualities of colour richness and surface texture. Many of the most rewarding effects of both painting and embroidery can be achieved, giving the advantage of an enormous range of possible uses.

The process of Thread Painting is still relatively unexplored and its potential yet to be fully appreciated. It is hoped that the introduction to the subject given in this book will inspire you to try your hand and to find your own original way of using it.

Thread Painting began as an amalgamation of the two disciplines of painting and embroidery. My interest in both these aspects of art came together several years ago in an attempt to produce some little embroideries with a pictorial content. In so doing, I started to look again at the known facts and techniques related to the two separate areas. There is a distinct overlap in the concepts involved. It has become apparent that it is possible actually to paint with threads, as an artist uses brushes and oils or watercolours, and that these effects are quite remarkable.

We are fortunate to live in an age and society which approves of, and encourages freedom of exploration in art. To a large extent, we are able to make the objects and pictures which please us, and to use a vast range of modern materials to achieve our aims. It is now acceptable to allow artists to expand their boundaries beyond the influences, fashions and expectations of established art forms, and to 'see' with a more analytical eye. This new medium of Thread Painting is, to some degree, the result of this adventurous attitude, but it can be used in a traditional, as well as an innovative way, depending on the individual taste of the artist.

Fabric and thread are materials almost exclusive to the embroiderer's or seamstress' skills. Recently, far-sighted artists have begun to examine more closely the quality of fabric and yarn, and to use them quite differently in their painting, sculpture and designs. The use of the sewing-machine is familiar within its intended domestic function, including the embroiderer's craft. Traditional use of canvas in painting is also an established practice. Thread Painting adapts that canvas foundation, substituting it for any suitable fabric, and by painting on it with any modern paints or dyes and introducing coloured sewing threads by machine stitching, it becomes a picture-making medium in its own right.

If you wish to try out the technique without great expense it is possible that you will be able to gather together all you need from family and friends. Many households have a swing-needle sewing-machine, which is sometimes idle for long periods. Here is a chance to put it to greater use. Anyone who likes dressmaking will surely be able to find a fair collection of part-used spools of sewing thread. There is no need to confine yourself to special embroidery threads, since dressmaking thread is produced in a far more extensive range of colours. If the seamstress in your family is a hoarder of part-used spools, she will also most probably have a store of useful bits of fabric left over from dressmaking. Paints, too, are often to be found in toy cupboards or attics, and children always seem to have a good supply of crayons or felt pens which you could use. All the essential requirements are standard items. You do not have to seek out specialist shops or to spend a great deal of money to make a start. As you become more skilful and enthusiastic, you can add to your stock of threads and paints. They are all readily available in most stores.

You will find Thread Painting a fascinating technique to use. It is possible to give your pictures a richness and spontaneity unique to this process. Machine stitchery enables you to work speedily or with precision, in response to your mood. Pictures made this way are especially effective, since the coloured threads have sheen and clarity, bringing a three-dimensional quality to the picture surface. They are as attractive to look at as to make, having the appearance of an oil painting at normal viewing distance, but the intriguing stitched effect on close inspection.

This book is intended as an introduction to the method and potential of Thread Painting. It will guide you through the practical and creative stages, and, above all, show you some of the exciting qualities you can achieve. The second section is devoted to a series of projects, which you might like to follow in preparation for designing your own pictures.

Painting is always a pleasant activity, and Thread Painting, with its particular characteristics, is especially absorbing. You are sure to find enjoyment in this new art form and to give pleasure to others through your pictures.

1

MATERIALS AND EQUIPMENT

Before you begin Thread Painting, check where you might find the necessary tools and materials. It is quite likely that you can begin without a special visit to the shops. You will see from the following list that all the requirements are normal items, which might initially be remnants of other hobbies, borrowed from friends, or invested in especially for Thread Painting when you grow more confident.

DOMESTIC SEWING-MACHINE

Any electric sewing-machine with a swing-needle (zig-zag) facility should be suitable for this work. Check that there is sufficient space to pass an embroidery hoop under the needle when no presser foot is attached. Establish also that the feed teeth (which guide the fabric from front to back in normal sewing) can be either lowered or covered up with a special plate. This allows you the essential freedom to move the picture about in any direction as you sew. Your machine does not have to be a sophisticated model. Built-in patterns and complex functions are not required since you, the artist, are going to control the machine's output.

If you have any doubts about the suitability or adaptation of your machine, you should seek the advice of your local stockist or service engineer. Ask him to demonstrate the setting up and use of the model as in 'free-hand darning or embroidery'. Also consult either expert if you feel that your machine needs servicing. Thread Painting should not harm it if you use it correctly, but there will certainly be more work for the machine than usual and it will need regular attention.

Some machines have a user's booklet which will guide you in the setting up and operating techniques. You will need a good supply of fine machine needles. Size 80 (UK size 12) or 70 (UK size 11) are recommended. Size 70 is the finest and most suitable for heavy density stitching since it passes easily through the work. However, needles tend to become blunt with use and sometimes break as a result of over-zealous sewing.

BACKGROUND FABRIC

Background fabric is the base upon which to build a Thread Painting and can influence the creative process. You should choose it carefully in relation to the type of picture you wish to make. It is important that you choose a good, firmly woven fabric that will stand the tensions and distortions that may occur when you apply heavy layers of stitching.

A fine fabric should be reinforced with an iron-on backing. It would be wise to experiment with this before starting your final picture since the performance of fabrics differ. There are some new types of vanishing muslin available from specialist needlework shops; they can be attached to a fine background material to firm it during use, but can be degraded later until they fall away from the finished work. 'Wet' methods of vanishing the muslin may not be suitable, but 'heat' methods would be more likely to succeed. You should take advice on the properties of the vanishing muslin.

The most suitable fabric background is a good quality unbleached calico (plain weave). It is reasonably inexpensive and has a pleasant canvas-like texture which is useful to paint on. Most of the illustrations in this book have a calico ground.

Calico is available in several widths and weights from dress fabric or furnishing departments of reputable stores. If you prefer a whiter form, ask for bleached calico.

PAINTS AND DYES

The first stage of work is the colouring of the fabric as a foundation for stitching. You will need some paints or colours which are water based. This enables

you to mix them freely, to dilute them easily, to wash your brushes thoroughly, and, above all, to dry the work quickly. Here are some suggested kinds of paints. Inventive folk may be able to add to my list by trial and error.

Acrylic Paints

Most of my work is done using this medium. Acrylic paints are thick like oil paints, but can be thinned down to use like watercolours. They have an exceptional permanence, which is important when your picture may hang in daylight for many years.

Acrylics are a modern form of plastic material, in an emulsion. They are mixable while wet from the tube, but once dried, will not wet up again. Do not leave this paint to dry on your brush. Spoilt brushes can only be restored in methylated spirit or brush-cleaning fluid and never really regain their original condition.

Acrylic paints are sold in tubes and are available in leading brands from all art material shops.

Watercolours

Both children's watercolour boxes and artist's quality paints are suitable for Thread Painting. You will find that they are rather thin and washy, unless you mix them heavily. Some watercolours have a more reliable permanence than others. This is not so important while you are just practising, but a treasured piece of work would be sadly lost if some of the colour faded.

Watercolours come in small rectangular containers or pans. These are dry blocks of pigment which have to be wetted with your brush. You can also buy them already moist in tubes. They are available from toy-shops (for children's paints) and art shops.

Fabric Dyes

There is now a wide selection of fabric dyes made especially for the purpose of painting on to materials of all kinds. Choose one that is water based.

You should check the labels or instruction leaflets for information about mixing colours, suitable fabrics to use them on, and about making them fixed or permanent. Most of these dyes come in jars and are available from art stores, craft suppliers and sometimes in shops supplying commercial artists.

Work in progress on the sewing-machine

Other Ideas for Background Colouring

Some paints not mentioned above may be suitable for your purpose. You should always try them out first to see if they work when stitching on top.

Inks are transparent colours and have great richness, but they can fade rapidly. Designer's gouache may work in certain styles of picture. You might like to try felt pens or fabric crayons for a very different effect.

> A short-cut to drying the painted fabric is often useful. Try to use a hand-held hair-dryer for swift and accurate drying.

SUGGESTED COLOUR RANGE

Whichever medium you wish to paint with, there is a minimum requirement for a satisfactory range of colours which will give you enough scope to mix the shades you need. Manufacturers will probably name each colour differently and will have a variety to choose from. The following list gives a basic range of essential colours and others which are likely to be most useful. It is then up to you to purchase more to improve the versatility of your palette.

The list gives a description of each colour and some of the likely names which manufacturers may use to describe a similar shade.

Essential Shades

White: Flake White, Titanium White, Chinese White and Zinc White are all useful. It is important to ask your supplier to assure you that the white you buy is 'bleed proof', ie that any colour mixed with it or lying under a layer of white will not rise to the surface and spoil the desired shade.

Yellow: If you inspect the maker's shade cards, you will see a variety of yellows. You should choose one which is not too orange in appearance. Lemon or Cadmium Yellow are suggested.

Red 1: As with other essential colours, choose a mid-red from the selection , ie one which is neither too orange nor too violet in appearance. Try Vermilion or Cadmium Red.

Red 2: In order to be able to mix a good range of purples, you will need this extra red. Try Rose, Carmine, Magenta or Crimson. You should note that some of these shades are less permanent and will probably be subject to fading. Check this with your supplier.

Blue: Use a good mid-blue from the range, such as Ultramarine or Cobalt Blue.

Additional Useful Shades

Purple: A mid-shade of violet such as Dioxazine Purple will prove valuable.

Greenish-blue: Look for a shade of blue with a bias towards green, such as Cerulean Blue and/or Prussian Blue, Monestial Blue or Indigo.

Reddish-brown: Try Transparent Brown, Burnt Sienna, Brick Red or Indian Red.

Neutral Brown: Use Raw Umber, Vandyck Brown or similar.

Extra Shades

There are other colours which may prove useful and be to your liking.

Viridian: A striking and brilliant green with many uses in mixing.

Hookers Green: A natural green with many uses in landscape work.

Gamboge or Indian Yellow: Rich earthy yellows both with warmth.

Chrome Orange: A vibrant orange.

There are, of course, many more for you to choose. My last piece of advice on the subject of colour selection is to avoid greys and black. This can only be a personal opinion, designed as a suggestion rather than directive. Totally neutral shades seem to deaden rather than enhance one's colour work. A near black or very dark shade can be mixed and it is likely to provide a richer effect than a black from a tube.

WOODEN EMBROIDERY HOOP

A range of simple wooden embroidery hoops (tambour frame) with a screw tightening mechanism and measuring from about 15 to 31cm (6 to 12in) is available in haberdashery departments or specialist needlecraft shops. You should choose one which is not too deep and will slip easily under the needle of your machine. My own hoops are about 1cm (½in) in depth. There is no need for anything more substantial.

You may wish to bind the inner ring with tape or bias binding to prevent the fabric slipping, especially if working with a fine background material.

It is advisable to choose the nearest size hoop to your piece of work. It avoids waste of surrounding fabric and enables you to see all of the picture within the framework of the hoop. Large pictures are difficult to make, particularly if you are a beginner, because you have to keep repositioning the hoop, working on just fragments of the whole picture at a time.

THREADS

You will need a range of coloured dressmaking threads. Standard polyester sewing yarn is most suitable for this purpose. Synthetic yarns are resistant to deterioration and have a good permanence of colour. I recommend Gütermann Sew All threads which I use throughout my work, as their colour range is excellent.

To start your collection of useful colours, sort into groups all your part-used spools left over from dressmaking projects. Often, you will find a predominance of colour in one or two areas, depending upon your taste in clothing or fashion trends. You could make a picture solely in these colour ranges or you could add to them to extend the shades.

As you work you will find the need to increase the shades available to you. You should aim to build up your coloured threads into as full a range as possible. Although polyester threads have been recommended here, natural yarns can also be used, but check first that they will not fade. Pictures are subjected to daylight at varying intensity and at much greater length than any garment. Daylight is harmful to textiles, causing fading, yellowing and deterioration. It is always a pity when a lovely piece of artwork needs extensive restoration. You never know how valued your pictures might be, even as family heirlooms. Do take extra steps to ensure that the materials you use are the most suitable for their purpose.

ADDITIONAL ITEMS OF EQUIPMENT

You will also need the following small items to equip yourself fully for Thread Painting:

◇ One or two soft painting brushes. Sable hair brushes are the finest quality but very expensive. There is now a good range of nylon brushes specially made for the artist, and you will find them pleasing to use but less costly. Choose various sizes and shapes, making sure that you have one which will be small enough for detail and one large enough to fill in wider areas of paint.

◇ A small pair of scissors for trimming the stitches. Curved nail scissors are ideal because you can trim close to the picture surface for a neat finish.

◇ A larger pair of scissors for cutting up your background material into the right sizes. Household or dressmaker's scissors will be suitable.

◇ Some pencils and rough paper, or cartridge paper, for early design work and for marking out designs on to the fabric.

◇ Tracing paper and transfer carbon (see Chapter 7).

◇ Needle and thread for stretching your picture when it is finished, and some strong flexible card upon which to stretch it.

◇ Water pot and palette, which can be as simple as a jam jar and white china saucer. Tissues or kitchen roll make excellent cloths for cleaning out brushes, palettes and wiping up accidental spills.

MOUNTING AND FRAMING EQUIPMENT

If you intend to mount and display your pictures yourself, you will need a good craft knife with plenty of spare blades. A surgical scalpel is very useful. To measure accurately, you will require a steel rule, a set square or protractor, a pair of compasses, a fine soft-leaded pencil, a good quality eraser and a cutting board. Professional cutting boards are available from art and craft shops, but if you wish to begin without great expense, you could use an offcut of mount card to protect your table-top, replacing it occasionally with a fresh piece.

You will want to select coloured mount card to suit each picture and to match a frame to the enhancement of the whole. Ready-made frames and mounts can be purchased from a picture-framing supplier. Alternatively, you could buy lengths of framing and special equipment to cut the 45° mitre which joins the corners neatly.

This last suggestion involves yet another set of skills and further expenditure. You may wish to leave it to the professional or to enlist the help of another member of your family or a friend who enjoys this aspect and with whom you could form a team.

It is suggested that you read through the chapters dealing with the method of Thread Painting, colour, texture, design and presentation before making any purchases. These sections of the book will tell you in more detail about the process and any alternative ways of working. They may help you to decide exactly which materials and equipment to buy and which extra items, such as tracing paper or framing, to put on your shopping list.

'Wind-pump at Seven Mile Point'

2
TECHNIQUE

Thread Painting is a process which comprises various distinct stages. While it is helpful to discuss these stages in clearly defined sections, the activity of Thread Painting is a united one, with the creative thought running from stage to stage as the picture progresses. Your picture should be allowed to develop and change while you work.

PREPARATION

First, you must have an idea for your picture and then you should choose a suitable background fabric which should be cut to a size 6cm (2½in) or more larger than the diameter of your embroidery hoop. You can leave it rectangular, even if you intend to do a circular picture. If the fabric is very fine or slippery, you may wish either to strengthen it with a backing material or to bind the inner ring of your hoop. Iron the fabric if it is very creased. Fit it into the hoop as follows:

1 Place the outer (larger) ring on the table-top and lay the fabric over it, with right side facing up.
2 Put the inner (smaller) ring on top, locating it inside the outer ring. Press it down firmly.
3 Gently adjust the fabric to keep the weave reasonably square, then tighten it in the hoop by means of the screw mechanism.

The work should remain this way up so that the fabric is always flat on the table-top and on the bed of the sewing-machine. It should always be kept taut like the skin of a drum to make stitchery easier.

PAINTING

The painting stage has several purposes. It is important as part of the creative process because it maps out the particular aspects of your design, establishes position, colour scheme, light and shade, and

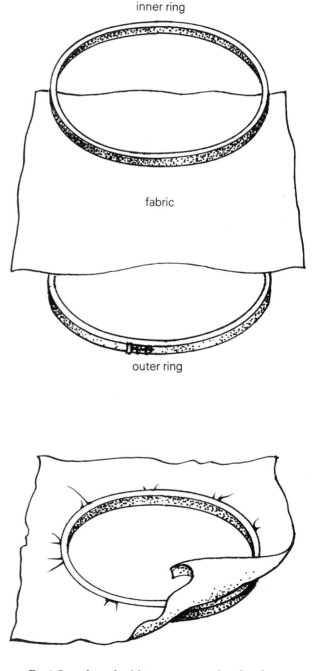

Fig 1 Stretching the fabric on to an embroidery hoop

suggests texture in the brush marks. Unplanned, but pleasing effects may occur during the painting. They can be retained or emphasised, giving your work a special air of spontaneity.

Painted fabric has an essential softening influence on the threads you will use later. Dressmaking thread is uniform and crisp. If you were to try stitching straight on to plain white fabric, you would probably spend much of your time trying to fill in all the little spaces between the threads because they show through and interfere with the colour you were hoping to achieve. Having painted your background with a similar colour to the threads you are using, it will not matter if you fail to cover it closely. In fact, you will learn to use this effect to your benefit.

Remember to think ahead and decide if any areas of your picture are going to be left largely unstitched. Most of your painting can be quite inexact and sketchy, but the parts you wish to leave will need to be painted fully at this stage.

To make a start, mark out your planned design on to the picture surface. Working with your fabric (now taut on an embroidery hoop) the right side up, pencil in the outer edges of the picture. Try not to work too closely to the hoop because your machine may not stitch properly near the wooden surround. Lightly sketch in the main features of your design, ready to add paint. Chapter 7 will give you further hints about methods of transferring this design to your fabric. If you are inexperienced, it would be useful to try out one or two of those ideas to find out which works best for you.

Without spending an unnecessary amount of time and energy on the drawing, start to put colour on as soon as you can. Your approach to using paints is sure to be individual, a matter for your own judgement. However, Chapter 4 will offer some simple suggestions on mixing and managing paint.

You should begin where and how you wish, but it is best to paint areas which are meant to appear distant before you put in objects that overlap them; and always make sure that the first part is dry before trying to paint neatly on top. For example, do paint the sky and dry it thoroughly before painting in the branches of a winter tree. It would be almost impossible to do the twigs first and have to paint bits of sky in between.

When painting the image, think carefully about the colour scheme you wish to achieve, and take trouble to get that and other aspects of the picture

just as you want them. Remember that this is your foundation for stitching. It should inspire you to add threads to embellish and improve the picture, but not restrict you too rigidly. Do not paint a masterpiece at this stage because you will be covering it up with threads later.

Many people will be familiar with the ready painted tapestry kits available in the shops and may even have worked them. There is a distinct danger of thinking of Thread Painting in the same way because of the apparent similarity in the stages. However, in Thread Painting you have the total freedom to create your own picture, to alter or follow your painting at will, to leave parts of the paint showing as an acceptable part of your work and to be as random or controlled with your stitches as you wish. Even the projects suggested later in this book can only be regarded as a series of starting points, because one cannot be expected to reproduce accurately the random stitches so rapidly created by the sewing-machine, and therefore no two pictures can be alike. Every piece of work will therefore be an original work of art.

SETTING UP THE SEWING-MACHINE

The electric swing-needle sewing-machine is to be your new painting tool. Like most apparatus, it needs some adjustment to improve its performance for a specific task. Your machine may have an instruction booklet giving useful diagrams to follow. Alternatively, you may need to seek professional advice about your particular model of machine.

The changes in setting that you will need to make are similar to those for 'free needle embroidery' or 'darning'. They are as follows:

1 The feed-dog, or apparatus with teeth, which protrudes through the needle plate, should be disengaged. In normal sewing these teeth guide the fabric through the machine at an even rate. The

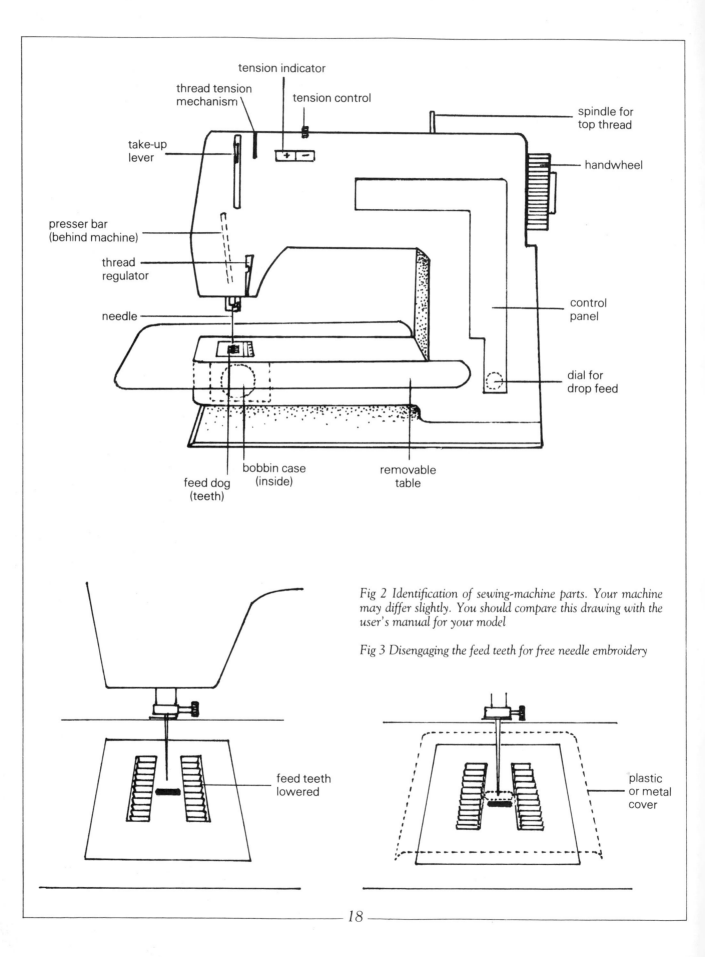

tension indicator

thread tension
mechanism

tension control

spindle for
top thread

take-up
lever

handwheel

presser bar
(behind machine)

thread
regulator

control
panel

needle

dial for
drop feed

feed dog
(teeth)

bobbin case
(inside)

removable
table

*Fig 2 Identification of sewing-machine parts. Your machine
may differ slightly. You should compare this drawing with the
user's manual for your model*

Fig 3 Disengaging the feed teeth for free needle embroidery

feed teeth
lowered

plastic
or metal
cover

effect of eliminating this facility is to allow free movement of the work in any direction. It also permits the user to pass the work to and fro under the needle at his or her desired speed, thus manually governing the stitch length.

Some types of sewing-machine have a switch which will cause the feed-dog to be lowered out of the way. Other models can be supplied with a plate attachment which clips over the feed dog to prevent it functioning. If you should not be able to make either of these alterations, it may be possible to unscrew the feed-dog and remove it completely.

2 Normally, the feed teeth operate in conjunction with a presser foot, and so in the absence of the feed you may also remove any regular presser foot. Thread Painting can be performed with no presser foot at all, but there are two important points always to observe. First, for the sake of safety, keep your fingers well away from the unguarded needle at all times and make a habit of removing your foot from the accelerator pedal each time you thread your needle. Secondly, always remember to lower the presser bar lever. In normal sewing this lowers the presser foot on to the fabric and also engages the top thread tension. It is all too easy to forget this simple action, but it is essential to begin stitching with tension operating correctly, even without any foot attachment.

It is possible that your machine may be fitted with a darning foot. This presser foot is designed especially for use without a feed-dog and can be a great help in Thread Painting. It enables beginners to be introduced to free machining without so much danger to fingers, as it acts as a guard by indicating where the needle will pierce the fabric. It also gives a more reliable stitch formation, holding the work more firmly and giving better control. Beginners often experience some difficulty in aiming the needle accurately. The darning foot seems to eliminate much of the insecurity of free needle sewing.

3 Set the tension of your machine. The tension of

the under-thread should not need adjustment from that of normal sewing. Slacken off the top thread tension just a little. In Thread Painting you will need to ensure that the under-thread never pulls through to the surface of your work during machining. You will be using the same under colour throughout to save bobbin changes. Diagram 4 shows you a correct stitch profile in both normal dressmaking and Thread Painting. You will see that, in the latter, the bobbin thread loops with the top one much nearer to the back of the fabric, reducing the risk of it showing above.

To check this tension setting for yourself, make a trial piece using contrasting coloured threads top and bottom. Set your zig-zag width to its maximum setting. Stitch a sample and look to see if the needle thread loops can just be seen under the fabric. Keep altering your needle thread tension until you are happy with the result. When you are using all the same brand and gauge of sewing thread throughout your picture, the tension should not need any alteration. If, however, you change your thread types, you may find it necessary to review the tension setting.

4 If you have a free-arm sewing machine you will find it more comfortable to fit the removable table to give you better support for your work.

5 Your machine will be doing a good deal of work. It is advisable to regularly oil the accessible parts and to brush away any accumulations of lint which may build up faster than usual. If you become a Thread Painting enthusiast, do have your machine serviced regularly. There are working parts which need maintenance by a qualified engineer. Your machine is the most valuable piece of equipment both in financial terms and to you as an artist.

Fig 4 Cross-section through fabric showing: 1 correct thread loop position in normal sewing; 2 loop towards the reverse of the fabric as it should be for Thread Painting

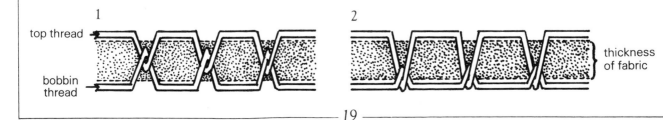

Figs 5–7 Exercises in stitch and texture control

Zig-zag setting O (running stitch)
Use for linear work

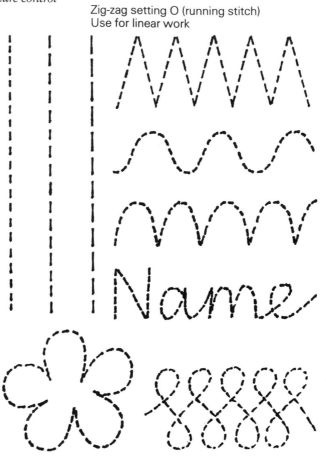

Zig-zag setting O. Very slow acceleration.
Join up dots with one long stitch

Filling in with running stitch

Zig-zag setting – narrow.
Practise loops, circles, dots and random texture

Zig-zag setting – medium.
Practise random textures, angled stitches and filling in shapes

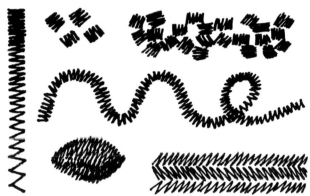

Zig-zag setting – maximum width.
Practise covering larger areas, angled stitching, and rocking from side to side

rotate your work

increase
zig-zag
manually

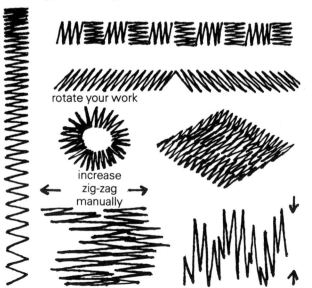

Zig-zag setting – altered gradually as you are stitching, from O to max and back again. (Only possible on sewing machines with manual zig-zag dial)

'Old Rectory Garden': first stage, in which the design is mapped out in pencil on to calico. The finished picture relies heavily on areas of light and shade, with texture, and the essential elements are already evident in the drawing

Second stage, taking the initial idea into paint, establishing the colour scheme and emphasising the dramatic lighting

Third stage, enlivening the painted calico with stitchery

The finished picture, mounted and framed

STITCHING THE PICTURE

You will be changing coloured needle threads as often as an artist mixes a new shade on his palette. Once you have become used to the threading up routine it will be no more inconvenient than that. There is no necessity to vary the colour of your under-thread. All you need to do is to wind two or three spare bobbins with your chosen base thread. A neutral colour such as beige or mid-grey would do as long as it is not too startling (just in case some traces of it become visible on the surface by mistake).

The picture, in its painted state, and still on the embroidery hoop, is slipped under the machine head the right way up. Remember that the fabric should be flat on the table of the machine with the rim of the hoop standing up around the picture. (In hand embroidery we are often taught to use the tambour frame the other way up, so do not get confused.)

Thread up your machine with your first chosen colour. Hold the end of the needle thread towards you and turn the wheel manually for one full cycle.

This will bring up the under-thread through your work. Lower the presser bar to engage the top tension. Holding both thread ends away from you, gently depress the accelerator pedal and make a few stitches. Cut off both ends as close as possible to the surface. You are now ready to stitch freely. This sequence is a useful one to practise until it becomes second nature.

Stitch Technique

Free machine stitching is a sensation that can at first be somewhat strange. Fortunately, once you have mastered the control of speed and steering, there is not a great deal more to learn. There are no special stitch formations to perfect and very few rules to follow. The only real constraints are the limitations of your sewing-machine. You will need to practise until you are familiar with the machine's performance and until you are competent enough to begin a simple picture. If you have experience of a sewing machine already, it will not take long for you to pick up the idea. To begin with, you could practise on a

piece of calico, perhaps even unpainted. Treat it like a doodle, while you get used to the freedom and speed of the technique.

Here are many of the possible shapes and textures that you can create with a zig-zag facility. Your machine may be capable of others and you may invent more for yourself.

Diagrams 5, 6 and 7 indicate the width of stitch from a straight running stitch setting through to your machine's maximum zig-zag setting, which may be up to approximately 5mm (¼in) wide. No stitch length settings are given because this machine function has been disengaged with the elimination of the use of the feed-dog. You govern the stitch length manually by the speed at which you pass the work under the needle. Leave your stitch length dial at '0' if you are in doubt.

The increased knowledge of your own potential will enable you to use a full repertoire of effects when picture making. In the section giving illustrated projects later in this book, reference is made to the above exercises to illustrate their usefulness.

Treat the above exercises as good experience, but allow yourself the luxury of making a picture as soon as you feel confident. Your enthusiasm will increase alongside your expertise, and you will be achieving more by using colour in a picture. Above all, do not feel that you have to go on practising for ages. Thread Painting is enjoyable and spontaneous.

Strategy for Stitching

To a large extent, how you go about working your picture depends upon your initial idea and upon your own creative individuality. However, there are some points which may be of help to you.

Sometimes it will be important to choose a suitable starting point. Your sequence of working will matter, for example, if your image features distance. The far-away hills should be sewn first, before you stitch in trees, buildings, and so on. A good discipline is to work from background, through middle distance to foreground. Fill in behind an object before you superimpose it. Work large areas if you can, before putting detail on top.

You may often be able to use the same coloured needle thread in several places on your picture, without spoiling your strategy for working. All you need to do is hop from one point to another and begin stitching again. Cut off the linking threads close to the work surface. There should be no need to trim the underneath threads. They will not be seen on the finished work and so do not matter.

You, the artist, decide which colours to use and choose the direction and texture of stitches. The picture can be developing all the time. Do not be afraid to alter it as you go along if it is necessary.

Mistakes can often be corrected by sewing over the top of them. You may occasionally have to unpick some of the stitches with your small curved scissors if the error is still going to show.

3
TEXTURE

The word 'texture' is frequently used to describe surface qualities in a work of art. It refers to the way a picture might feel if we were to touch it and to the remarkable ability we have for estimating that feeling, just by looking at it.

Thread Painting is, in essence, a way of applying special textures to a picture surface, making it an exciting medium to work in.

There are four main aspects to consider while you work, in order to use texture to its greatest potential: scale, shape, movement and light sources.

Fig 8 Texture and detail reduce in size towards the distance

SCALE
If your painting is any way representative of a real object or scene, it is sensible to use the best size and scale of stitches to suit the image. For example, if your picture features a flower garden in which there are two lilac bushes, one in the distance and one in the foreground, the effect would be more realistic if the distant bush were done in small stitches, but the nearer one stitched more boldly. This is an attempt to follow what our eyes actually see. Artists often use this convention, which is part of a theory called perspective, in which objects appear to diminish in size the further they are from the eye.

'High Summer': this picture required careful planning of the available space. The pencil sketching stage involved choosing a good proportion of sky and land, and also the placing of the dominant tree so that it divided up the picture space pleasingly and formed an interesting series of sky patches in conjunction with the picture's own outline

The painting stage developed the important aspects of colour, and light and shade, conveying the feeling of summer heat

The stitching began in the distance, with tiny texture and working forward through the scene. In this illustration, the main tree is part-finished. The next step will be to add leaf effect over the framework of branches and to make a good outline to the canopy

Detail of 'High Summer'

The resulting picture, featuring foreground dappled shadows and close-up grassy texture

You could also use varying scales of texture: bold, thick, chunky, or thin, dotted, fine marks, in an abstract way. Contrasts or gradual changes in texture are sufficient alone to make a picture more interesting. Together with colour variety and skilful planning, they can make an extremely useful contribution to your creative expertise.

The scale of stitches you choose to work in will also reflect how you feel about your subject matter. Tight, small and precise texture would suit an image with plenty of detail, the sort of picture which will make you study it over and over again to appreciate its content; whereas broad, random strokes full of sweeping lines and patches may give the impression that the artist has responded with joy, anger or enthusiasm to his subject, and wishes you to share the impact of what he saw.

SHAPE

An artist will often use directional strokes of his brush, pen, or pencil quite deliberately for different purposes. If, for instance, the object being painted was rounded, like gently rolling hills, he might allow his brush strokes to curve as he paints, in the undulating configuration of the landscape. He would be thinking with his painting along the contours of his subject.

You, too, could do this in Thread Painting both with the paint and stitch stages. Let the texture you use echo characteristic shapes in your work. Try the following exercise for yourself on a piece of scrap paper to see what is meant:

Draw two separate circles. On one circle make a perfectly straight line of small dots (like running stitch) across from one side to the other. On the second circle, make your dotted line curved as it goes from side to side. Ask your friends or family which circle looks flat and which rounded like a sphere.

Also, you could copy the texture of animal fur as it follows the contours of the creature's body, or markings of bark on a twisted tree trunk, and so on, using your stitch direction to explain shapes in your picture.

MOVEMENT

In much the same way you could make your textures even more expressive by indicating movement. The

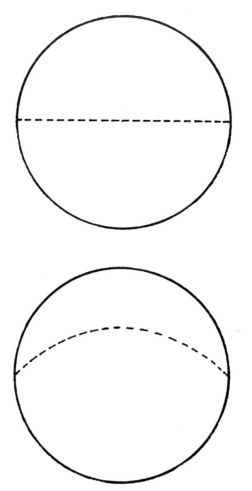

Fig 9 These two circles are the same. Which one looks flat and which appears three-dimensional?

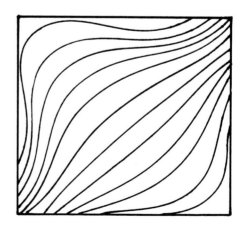

Fig 10 Wavy lines drawn across the square give the illusion of a bulge in the surface, overriding our reasoning which tells us that the surface is, in fact, flat

clearest example is an open field of standing corn. Normally this could be interpreted as regimented ranks of vertical texture, but if the wind blew across the field, the stalks of corn would bend and sway, rippling with movement. Stitch direction would have to vary to express this.

As with all changes of direction when sewing, you will be obliged to twist and turn the work to make stitches form how and where you want them.

LIGHT SOURCES

When light plays on the surface of textured work it accentuates the three-dimensional quality. This is especially so with the use of domestic sewing threads which have an inherent regularity and sheen. The effect changes if you move the source of light so that it falls from an alternative direction.

The following experiment could be fun to try:

Make a little abstract picture and divide the surface up into odd shapes using plenty of variations in texture, but only one colour. It might surprise you to see just what can be achieved using this technique. Observe the changes which occur when the light falls at different angles. One of these changes can be particularly useful. Notice that a patch of regular zig-zag stitches looks pale if the light comes from one angle. That same patch appears much darker if you move the light source round 90°.

The combination of light and texture may be one feature of Thread Painting that has attracted interest in the medium. Such pictures seem to have an elusive liveliness which is perhaps due to this effect.

The description of the Thread Painting technique described here concentrates largely on aspects directly related to that medium. The possibilities are widened even more by amalgamation with other related methods and materials. You could add further texture by couching in other yarns such as chenille, bouclé wools, string or metallic thread. The inclusion of appliquéd pieces of cloth, hand stitching or beads may suit your picture. You could even turn the whole sequence upside down, by using bits of Thread Painting as an inclusion in a pre-dominantly hand-worked piece.

4
COLOUR

The making of a Thread Painting will almost certainly involve the use of colour at both the preparation and stitching stages. Sensitive and well-planned colour schemes are vital components of any artistic work. Colour can be employed for all sorts of purposes. It can express mood, weather conditions, light and shade, movement and depth. Colour theory is a complex and fascinating scientific topic which may be studied in greater depth by further reading.

Many people express their hesitance to begin Thread Painting because of their inexperience in, or dislike of, using paints. It may be that you have not painted for some years and unhappy memories of early attempts have deterred you ever since. This chapter is intended as an easy guide to help you with colour mixing and applying paints. It will also deal with using coloured threads in machining.

The two most common difficulties concern the problems of mixing the right colour and with making paint behave as you want it to on paper (or in this case, the fabric). These are purely technical problems and can easily be overcome with a little practice.

Later in this chapter there are a few suggested exercises to do in sequence and to keep as notes for reference. You could make them in the form of a chart to help you look up a colour and its mixing formula. You also need to know a little about colour theory.

Colours come from rays of white light emitted by the sun. A beam of light can be split up into a rainbow (called the visible spectrum), by using a crystal or prism. Rainbows seen in the sky are the result of light rays from the sunshine being split up by the many tiny droplets of water in a damp atmosphere.

Light rays divide up into the visible spectrum when passed through a prism

Detail of 'Old Rectory Garden'

Scientists explain the colour that we see on the surface of all objects in the following way. Objects actually absorb some of the components of white light from the sun's rays, but reflect the rest. For example, a blue flower is absorbing all the colours of the rainbow except blue. The blue part of the spectrum is reflected back and is received by the human eye. White clothing is a cool colour to choose to wear in hot countries because it reflects all the visible parts of the sun's rays, whereas black garments absorb so much light that they reflect virtually none of the brightness and warmth which we associate with sunshine.

Artists' paints are made with very finely ground powders of coloured material called pigments, which are bound together with various gums or liquids. These pigment particles reflect light in the same way as other solid objects.

Paints can be mixed to produce any colour the artist requires, following a few simple rules.

PRIMARY COLOURS

There are three colours in the spectrum that are original: pure red, blue and yellow. These are the primary colours and they cannot be mixed by combining paints of any two or more other colours. You must buy them ready made from manufacturers who produce them chemically.

Always mix your paint thoroughly on a palette before using it. Thick paints are best mixed with a palette knife so that all the grains of colour are evenly distributed. Patches of unmixed colour tend to stick among the bristles of a brush and appear as streaks when the brush is used.

Always keep your brushes, palette and water clean, especially when you require an accurate colour mix. Tiny amounts of unwanted colour will spoil the clarity of your intended shade. Clean brushes that have been used for acrylic paint extra well, because once it dries it cannot be removed in water.

SECONDARY COLOURS

The three primaries are the basis for mixing all other colours. Mixing just two primaries together in any proportions gives you intermediate colours called secondaries. They are greens, oranges and violets. You could begin your colour chart by making a copy of the colour wheel shown on p34. All other mixing is based on it.

TERTIARY COLOURS

By mixing all three of the primaries in varying proportions, a whole range of browns and neutral colours is obtained. To make any shade lighter you can either water it down or mix it with a small quantity of white. Black paint is actually manufactured, but a near match can be made by the artist by careful mixing of accurate quantities of the three primaries. However, black is a poor colour to choose if you wish to make any other colour darker. It tends to deaden the result. Use another dark colour instead. Try mixing it with purple, which often gives a pleasing richness to a painting.

In Chapter 1 there is a list of useful colours to buy and some are stressed as essential. Using these, plus any other shades you happen to have, follow the next sequence of mixing schemes and add them to your colour wheel diagram.

MIXING SECONDARY COLOURS

Exercise 1
On paper, copy the chart on page 34 using two primary colours only.

1 Put a little yellow on your palette.
2 Paint some of it in a patch about 2cm (1in) square, using either a brush, or a palette knife if you are using thick paint.
3 On your palette, mix a tiny amount of red into the yellow. It should turn slightly orange.
4 Paint a sample of this orangey yellow next to the yellow.
5 Add a little more red to the yellow on the palette and paint another sample on your chart.
6 Do this several more times so that you have a chart ranging from yellow through oranges in even stages.
7 Lastly, paint a sample of pure red.

You will see that the exercise has already given you a range of colours which you could use in painting.

Exercise 2
Using blue and red, repeat Exercise 1.

Exercise 3
This time, use yellow and blue to repeat Exercise 1.

> *You will notice that paint manufacturers produce more than one kind of red, blue and yellow. It is important to try out several kinds when doing mixing experiments. This is particularly true when mixing red and blue together. The combination is supposed to make purple. Some reds are too orange biased, and some blues too green to make a pleasing purple. Try with Ultramarine and a Crimson or Magenta for reasonable results.*

MIXING TERTIARY COLOURS

Exercise 4
Opposite each other in the colour wheel on p34 you will find one primary and one secondary colour. These opposites are called complementary colours and have a contrasting effect upon one another. Mixing these opposites gives a wide range of less recognisable shades, called tertiary colours. These more subtle colours are very useful in painting and form the basis of every other shade you will wish to make.

1 Choose a pair of opposites, for example yellow and purple.
2 As with the first three exercises, start with one colour in its purest form. Add small quantities of its opposite and paint a sample of each new shade on to your chart.
3 At each stage, you might like to take a small quantity of the new colour and mix it with a little white paint. Paint a sample next to its original.

This will show you the effects of making the mixture paler and could prove a useful reference.
4 Finally, paint a sample of the opposite colour in its pure form.

Exercises 5 and 6
Repeat Exercise 4 with blue/orange and then with red/green.

Exercise 7 (optional)
You might like to try mixing similar sample strips with random pairs of other colours from your painting set. This is an extra exercise which might seem unnecessary, but it will tell you a good deal about the mixing properties of your own collection of colours. It will prove invaluable to know what to expect from any combination. Liken it, if you can, to a good cook who knows from experience the likely results of blending several ingredients in a recipe.

When you have completed these exercises, you should have a useful chart which can be referred to whenever you wish to make a special colour. Look for the nearest shade. You will be able to see which pair of colours was used to mix it and in roughly what proportions. You can always make it paler by adding more white. You will quickly recognise the need to adjust the colour slightly for a perfect match.

USE OF COLOUR

In its simplest form, painting in colour is just like a copying process. By matching your colour mix to the corresponding part of the subject matter and painting it in accurately, you can make a good representation on paper. In the same way, but mechanically, a camera records the instantaneous image on film. To be able to do this in paint and by your own visual judgement is no mean feat. If you acquire this skill through practice, you are already well equipped to be an acceptable artist.

Thinking deeper about the subject of colour, you will come across more subtle aspects which could influence its use in painting. You could loosely call them colour effects.

Mood
We are all familiar with the expressions which refer to a colour, usually defining a particular mood. For example, we say 'in a blue mood' to mean forlorn,

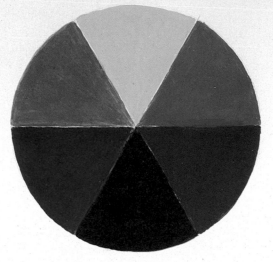

*The colour wheel and
paint-mixing charts*

The effects of complementary colours: in the red-green diagrams, you can see for yourself how the colours jostle for position. If you focus on the joins between the colours, they should appear to fight for dominance

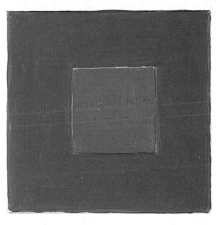

Study the blue-orange samples to see the same effect, but ask yourself which of the inner squares appears to recede, and which come forward

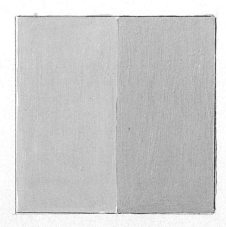

In order to make yellow and purple have any complementary effect on each other, they must be brought as close as possible in tone. Purple is a very dark colour and must be made much paler

The last example shows two colours which, on their own, look grey. Brought into contact with each other, the slight red bias of one maximises the small amount of green in the other and vice versa

depressed or sad; or 'looking at life through rose-tinted spectacles' to signify that a pink overall bias improves one's perception of any situation. More generally, we use the saying that a single occurrence 'coloured our opinion' of an event. Clearly, we mean that colours have a special influence on our attitudes and behaviour. These psychological and traditional concepts can be exploited by the artist to send underlying messages of mood to the viewer of his or her picture.

Try it out for yourself. Shut your eyes to imagine two pictures, one of them happy and the other full of mystery. Now make a conscious attempt to record in your mind the general colour schemes in both pictures. Ask other people to do the same and compare your opinions.

If you look at two pictures in the series of projects, 'Poppy Field' and 'Sunset' on pp107 and 118, you will see that they are quite similar in their simple portrayal of landscape during summer. However, by varying the general colour scheme, each has an identifiable mood, linked to our understanding of midday sun and failing daylight.

Weather

Climatic conditions cause changes in the overall colour of any view. The reader may be able to imagine the bright saturated colours of a Mediterranean scene, with rocks, sea and white stucco houses with red roofs, then to compare that intensity of colour with a view of the Scottish Highlands with their soft heather and mist shades.

Even if you were to study just one view and record the changes of weather and seasons, there would be plenty of interesting material for several paintings. These changes in what we see mainly occur because of differences in the angle of the sun, amounts of daylight and of water droplets in the air. Some artists have found this study fascinating and rich in source material. The English painter Joseph Turner, who worked at the beginning of the nineteenth century, was famous for his strong swirling pictures of atmospheric content.

Light and Shade

The tonal values of colours, or their brightness or darkness, can be used to show the three-dimensional shapes of objects. Black and white photographs show the areas of light and shade in a picture. They simplify any view to a scale of tones ranging from white, through gradually darkening greys, to black.

In a colour picture those greys and blacks have a colour richness as well as a tone. To demonstrate this, take a good look at a familiar object, such as an orange. It is easy to see that it has a light and a dark side where the shadow falls. We all know that an orange is usually that one colour all over, but to paint a picture of it, we must alter the brightness of that colour. The darkest part will need to be painted a deep rust shade (a rich, dark version of orange).

When composing a picture, do not forget to have the light coming from the same direction on to all the constituents of the painting. Highlights and shadows usually come from one light source and illuminate objects at the same angle.

Movement

The optical effects of certain colour combinations can be remarkable. If you intend to make abstract images, this aspect of colour theory may be of extra interest. There is a good deal of experimentation that you could do with reference to a fully detailed study book about colour.

Here are just a few instances to illustrate this concept. Taking the complementary pairs of colours and making them similar in tone, you could paint them alternately in intricate waves and stripes, or even a chequer-board pattern. Complementary colours have the capacity to exaggerate the richness of their partners. Red looks more red when next to green and vice versa. A long stare at the join between red and green patches will give you the impression that they are jostling for position. Even if present in very small amounts, the opposites will affect each other. Pale grey with a mere hint of green and another with a touch of red will both look grey, unless they are brought together. Side by side, the greenness and the redness are enhanced by the nearness of their complementaries.

Some colours can appear to be nearer to the picture plane, while others seem to recede. It is often said that colours fight or clash with one another. Occasionally, it becomes fashionable to wear daring colour combinations. Artists have sometimes used such phenomena in their work.

How and why you choose to use colour groupings for their unusual effects is a matter for you to decide. Your picture may even make a feature of these eye-catching ideas.

Perspective

The principles of drawing perspective are a guide to making the distances between objects seem realistic on paper. Mostly they concern drawing and are described more fully on pp 61–3.

The use of colour and tone is often overlooked as a means of depicting space from distance to foreground. The theory concerns the changes brought about by atmospheric conditions on the natural colour of objects. Moisture, dust and heat in the air soften down colours. The further they are away from you, the more the intervening atmosphere subdues their richness. It has become a cliché to describe distant hills as blue or mauve, but it is often accurate.

As with many of the points raised in this book, it is a good idea to take a purposeful look around and observe them for yourself. The exercise will increase your knowledge and awareness of the visual world. If you are an enthusiastic photographer, you could do this with a view to collecting your own library of useful pictures for reference. A scrap book of cuttings, postcards, and so on, featuring images that inspire you, is a good alternative.

CONTROLLING PAINT

Inexperienced painters might like to try the following suggestions to improve their handling of paint both on paper and fabric.

Exercise 8

During an early term at art school, my respected tutor remarked to me that my choice of brush was inadequate for the task in hand. He likened my progress to 'eating soup with a fork'.

The following exercise should help you to know more about the range of performance of your brushes and help you to predict the suitability of each for various parts of your painting.

1 Choose several different types and sizes of brush with which to experiment.
2 Mix up some paint with water until it is quite fluid, or you can use ink.
3 Using each brush in turn, try out its performance on paper, and again on fabric similar to that which you intend to use in Thread Painting. (It is best to put the fabric on an embroidery hoop.) Use the brush sideways, upright, squashed firmly down; make it form dots, lines, squiggles, neat marks, large patches and, letting it run short of paint, make dry fuzzy marks. Note in your mind which brush performs best at any particular task. Later, when you are doing proper painting, you will need to pick the right brush for the job.

Exercise 9

1 On paper and fabric, paint crisp lines and dense patches with a brush loaded with any colour.
2 Dry these marks thoroughly.
3 Now paint carefully up to and around these marks with another colour. You should produce neatly touching patches of colour which have crisp edges. They should not have run or smudged.
4 Try putting dabs of thicker paint on top of the previous colours, again without smudging or running.

Exercise 10

1 Wet the paper or fabric with a clean brush and clear water.
2 Allow paint of several colours to run into the wet patches. The damp background will allow them to mingle. You will not achieve crisp neat edges whenever the background or neighbouring areas are still damp.

Artists call this wetting and blending process 'putting on a wash'. It can be used deliberately to ensure a smooth all-over effect as in a sky. It is also effective when you wish to have a gentle transition from one colour to another, as in the blush of a cheek, or light into shade.

These last three exercises were designed to show you how to bring about particular qualities and to enable you to use them to advantage.

'South Walsham Wood' invites the viewer to wander from one woodland glade to another. Its feeling of tranquillity is enhanced by the use of soft blue-greens, which become misty and delicate in the clearing. The scene has a stage-set quality. The nearest groups of trees are seen in detail, whereas those in the distance could be a backdrop. Similarly, the light falls from above, illuminating the glade beyond

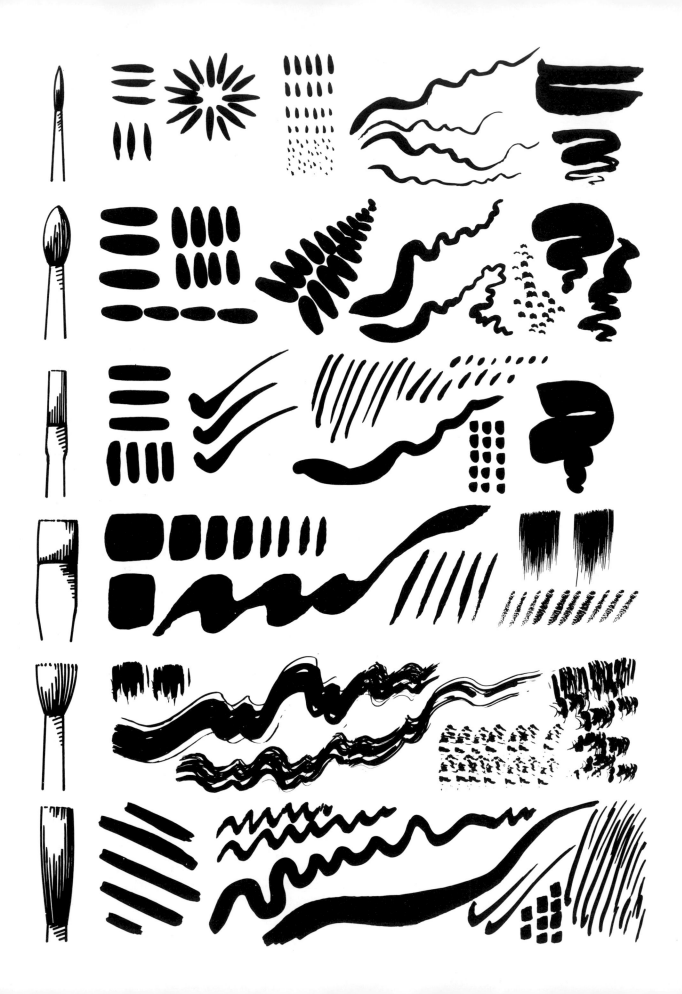

It is possible that much of the creative activity which we call art is the ability to take accidental effects, having observed how they came about, and to use them purposefully. I am sure this is true of some aspects of Thread Painting. You will see for yourself by close inspection of the illustrations in this book that much of the work looks random. It is only an impression and not by any means an accurate rendering of the subject matter.

USING COLOURED THREADS

At the beginning of this chapter, colour mixing was discussed with a view to achieving the exact shade in paint. Threads are, of course, unchangeable self-colours and cannot be mixed in the same way as paint. Therefore, they must be used in an entirely different way.

First, you will need to collect together the fullest possible range of threads, encompassing your picture's colour scheme. The image will be improved in depth and richness if you include threads of light and dark tones, plus some which seem marginally too strong and bright, but which belong to the general colour group. They might not be used in great quantity, but judicious touches here and there can give a Thread Painting extra sparkle.

If you cannot obtain threads of just the right colours, you can achieve them by stitching a blend of more than one shade of fairly close match to the one you require. The result of mingling near shades, from a normal viewing distance, is usually satisfactory and often pleasing to look at because of its variety. If you allow the background paint to show through between the stitches, this too can help soften the appearance of a poorly matched colour.

The fact that threads cannot be mixed like paints, but remain their own true colour, is not such a drawback as it seems at first. Indeed, it is probably one of the most important qualities of Thread Painting which distinguishes it from other painting media. This unimpaired colour gives the resulting work a particularly rich, vibrant appearance.

When an artist is working in a mixable medium, such as watercolours or oil paints, there is always the risk that each newly mixed shade will become dull and muddy because of the presence of misjudged amounts of pigment (see your experiments in colour mixing, p32). Also, every time a good accurate colour is applied to the painting, there is a likelihood that it will smudge or blur even slightly with shades already on the canvas or paper. The results, however carefully done, might show signs of this reduction in colour clarity.

Around the end of the nineteenth century, a group of artists whom we call the Impressionists became aware of the need for purity of colour in painting. Their emergence as an innovatory group came about partly as a response to the improving methods of early photography, which made them conscious of hitherto unobserved visual effects. Among these was the phenomenon of captured instants in time and vision. Until that era, painters had largely portrayed an amalgamation of what they had seen over longer periods.

The work of the Impressionists freshly explored the behaviour of light and colour. Their pictures are recognised for their brighter, almost luminous colour bias. Some artists even went to the extreme of applying dots and patches of clear bright paint, without attempting to smooth them in on the canvas or blend them in any way. A close-up examination of these pictures shows only unintelligible blobs, but from a normal viewing distance, the eye takes in the overall appearance of these carefully arranged colour patches and interprets them as a recognisable shape.

There is a direct comparison to this in nature. If you look at a highly magnified view of a butterfly wing, you will see that it is made up of overlapping coloured scales which give it that wonderful soft glowing quality and distinctive pattern. These vibrant colours are difficult to copy in paint. However, Thread Painting is a medium with some comparable qualities.

A close inspection of the surface threads gives the impression of a random jumble of unrelated lines in coloured thread. The result at a proper distance is surprisingly realistic. The threads retain their own luminosity, but combine in the perception of the viewer to form a coherent image. Over and above this quality, the texture and surface sheen contribute further to the attractiveness of Thread Painting.

Using the sewing-machine and domestic dressmaking thread to produce a pictorial effect is most closely comparable with the crayoning process. In

Fig 11 Different types and sizes of brush have their own distinct characteristics. Experiment like this with your own brushes to get to know their potential

'Immortals': this abstract picture uses the complementary qualities of the blue and orange range. Its subject matter was developed from some ancient glazed tiles in a mural, but it was the restricted colour scheme in conjunction with the part-random, part-geometric pattern that inspired me. I have retained from the original only the aspects which pleased me most. The painting stage was free and enjoyable, without obligation to follow the theme too closely. I had fun stitching the picture and was able to adapt the painted canvas at will, while echoing the wonderfully lustrous colours of the tiles themselves in sewing threads

'Cucumber Corner': portrayal of the English landscape involves extensive use of greens. This picture shows how you might make the most of a collection of threads largely limited to one colour group. It relies on variations within that range, including light and dark shades

reality, the sewing-machine makes only thin lines or zig-zags. If you ask any child to mime the action of crayoning, he or she will inevitably make a similar side to side movement with the hand. Children use crayons to draw lines or to colour in larger patches by an intensive scribbling motion over the same area until the colour is applied uniformly. They can work roughly and with great flourishes, or neatly with much more control. The only fundamental difference is that the crayon is a movable tool. In Thread Painting the tool is static, but the picture must be guided with some accuracy. If you are familiar with using a sewing-machine for any purpose, this concept should be quite natural, but if you are approaching Thread Painting for the first time, you will need to be more conscious of the guidance process for a while.

If you feel that you would like to practise to familiarise yourself with some of the ways that coloured thread can be used, try this next exercise.

Exercise 11

1 With your background fabric (preferably calico) stretched taut on an embroidery hoop, pencil a circle about 2cm (1in) in from the edge of the hoop to mark an outer limit to your work. Divide the circle into four separate areas, in any arrangement you wish.
2 Paint these areas in the following manner:
a) Small patches, stripes, etc clearly and crisply. Use a special colour scheme.
b) In another colour scheme, make much broader patterns.
c) Wet this area with clean water. Using bright colours, blend in several shades so that the colours remain clear, but each one merges smoothly into the next in the same way as the colours of the rainbow. Dry this section before going on.
d) Again, wet this last area and blend in shades of one colour only, ranging from its lightest to its darkest tone.
3 Now try following your painted foundation in threads on your sewing-machine.

You will be obliged to find ways of preserving or accentuating the painted effects in thread. In doing so you will develop your own style. The result will be a useful sampler for the future.

Incidentally, your exercise might be sufficiently attractive to put in a frame and to display as your first 'abstract'.

5
SOURCES OF INSPIRATION

Any kind of picture-making involves the introduction of a good deal of creative style natural to the individual artist. It is possible that you will have your own opinion of the type of picture you wish to produce. Images seen in other media may well have an influence. You may be an accomplished painter with an established style. Those who have a firm working plan ready to put into action will need little guidance.

However, for some the task of finding a suitable source idea for a picture is a daunting prospect. With all the world of sights and experiences to choose from, it is often difficult to narrow down the selection to a useful starting point. This section is intended to make it easier for you to examine the possibilities and to help you develop a picture from a source.

To avoid a wide directionless search for inspiration, ask yourself what sort of image you would most enjoy making. Do you find that landscapes appeal to you? Have you an interest in wildlife? Would you prefer to look at a garden, still-life or abstract framed and hanging on your living-room wall? Do you respond to bright or subtle colours? Think around your own areas of knowledge, such as the characteristics of the environment in which you live or to which you regularly return for holidays. You may have a fascinating hobby like stamp collecting, angling or gardening. Whatever your special interests or experience, these could be an excellent starting point for Thread Painting images, because you already have first-hand knowledge of the subject and will be able to put depth of information into your picture.

The illustration entitled 'Damgate Marsh' on p46 depicts a favourite theme of mine, reflecting a typical aspect of the region of Norfolk in which I live. It is inevitable that much of my work is influenced by the East Anglian landscape, and this picture of the Halvergate marshland, with its lush growth of reeds punctuated by clusters of aged willow trees, was painted after walking there on a bright summer morning. With the sensations still fresh in my mind and plenty of previous experience of that place, which is my frequent choice for a walk, I painted and stitched quite spontaneously. The picture is one which still recalls much of the feeling of the place and has prompted similar response from others who know and love the marshes. I am rarely satisfied with any of my pictures, but because this image appears to succeed in communicating my impressions to others, I can allow myself pleasure in it. Certainly, my first-hand knowledge of the subject matter is contributory to its success even if the picture itself is a dilute version of reality.

Any picture which really holds the onlooker's attention is almost certain to have been painted by someone who thoroughly knows about his subject. For instance, a portrait which is said to have caught the likeness of the sitter can only have been achieved through a genuine rapport between artist and model. A picture of a bowl of roses will probably be quite recognisable if painted from memory, but will be far more convincing if the artist actually looks at and records the unique twists and curls of the real thing. It will be better still if they are his favourite flowers and if he is a rose expert.

You should make an effort to draw from life if possible, or to use photographs and other visual references, rather than relying on the already diluted information stored in the memory.

The assessment of an idea should be based on your intuitive enthusiasm for the subject and should also take into account some practical points.

First, be sure that your chosen subject matter lends itself to the technique. A straightforward picture of a well-known cathedral with all its complicated architectural features might be best attempted in pen and ink, with which you could be precise and controlled. On the other hand, a run-

down country cottage, with uneven shapes, untidy thatch or leaning walls, might be more suited to Thread Painting. Look for plenty of texture, colour schemes and something lively in its character.

The picture 'White Cottage' on p79 illustrates the inclusion of an architectural feature in a compostion with the minimum of commitment, while using to advantage its suitability to Thread Painting. The texture in its thatching ideally lends itself to the stitch marks and the crisp white painted walls offer a contrasting smoothness, plus an opportunity to include the evidence of bright sunshine and shadow. By hiding most of the complicated features of the building behind holly and weeping willows, the necessity for accurate detail has been avoided. The image, instead, makes a feature of the white and green of cottage, trees and the grassy banks with ox-eye daisies, all of which are easily translated into stitch.

Secondly, the subject matter should have some special quality which you think is worthwhile trying to convey to the viewer. If you wish to paint an out-standing scene, ask yourself what makes it particularly noteworthy. A picture of your family pet could portray the appealing way in which he always attracts your attention, or the charming but naughty habit he has of chewing slippers. The view from your window might be especially pretty at evening time, when the sun is low, shedding a golden light, but not so remarkable under an overcast sky. Your work will be successful if you design it with a special aspect in mind.

The contents of 'High Summer' on p27 show a relatively featureless landscape, which would probably make a weak, uninteresting image if portrayed on a rainy day, without sun or shadow, or at a time

'On Damgate Marsh': light and shade effects have been used in two ways in this picture. The literal interpretation of shade can be seen in the darkness of the overhanging willow and in the shadow it casts in the otherwise brightly lit landscape; the sunshine is coming from the left-hand side. This heaviness in the foreground gives importance to the tree and emphasises the jewel-like colours in the distant view beneath its branches.

Tonal variations in the colouring of the dry reeds gives shape to an otherwise flat landscape. The foreground shows a strong change in the contours, suggesting a dip down into an over-grown ditch. This effect is brought about by shading which depicts shape.

of year when the fields had just been ploughed. I chose to record this view particularly for its feeling of strength of summer sun, its powerful shadows, and the proud, shapely oak tree standing guard over the dry wheat fields. It is my hope that it communicates a sense of relief from the sun's glare while standing in the foreground shade, and an air of expectancy that, if one was to set off walking down the road to the distance, the heat would be engulfing as soon as one left the shade.

'Water Garden' illustrated on p70, makes a particular feature of water-lilies, as their shiny leaves catch the light and form a pattern against the darkened waters of the lake. I have enlarged the image until that is almost the only recognisable element in the work, except for the evidence of rushes in the foreground and waterside plants at the far bank. These extra details help to identify the subject matter and to hold the composition together.

We are all inclined to be over-critical of our own work and sensitive to comparisons with the achievements of others. Do try to remember that the word 'criticism' refers to the act of assessing merits as well as finding faults. Always look for the best attributes, and if faults must be found, think positively about how to avoid them and correct them in your next work. It would be a great pity if they were allowed to cloud your enjoyment.

Thirdly, you should try to decide in advance if the chosen subject is within your capabilities. If it entails too much detail, difficult drawing or ambitious effects, you may be disappointed and discouraged. These decisions are best made for yourself and in complete self-honesty. We all have to start learning a new technique gradually and to make mistakes and have successes in stages. This aspect of learning, of becoming proficient in any activity, is so important. It helps if you can seek the encouragement of others.

Young children are often most successful in their attempts to use new media because they do not naturally show sensitivity about their own degree of skill or talent. They just proceed with an idea and enjoy its making. They are capable of accepting some attempts as poor, erasing them from memory and trying again.

The children's work on pp90–1 is the result of only a few minutes' instruction about this new technique and a first or second try on a sewing-machine. The youngest child was nine-years old. Their pictures are a response to the vibrance of colours, the rapid output of the machine and pleasure in picture-making. None were inhibited by their experience and each was enthralled by the process.

Thread Painting is a freely creative process. The best advice to a beginner is to proceed in manageable stages and to allow plenty of scope for success. Look with pride upon the best features of each new work.

SUBJECT MATTER

Developing an idea for a picture will involve a combination of your own tastes and interests and an input of fresh information. You should begin by investigating within a restricted field and by collecting mental notes along with the visual material. Subject matter for works of art falls into several categories.

Landscapes

Traditional subjects are bound to be high on the list for selection. Although they have been used time and time again, they never fail to please. There is always a new picture to be made from an old theme. Your own individual preferences, perception and style will produce a work with freshness, so do not be afraid to start with a deliberate attempt to copy. You will not be content to do so for long and will soon begin to modify the image to suit yourself.

Throughout history, landscapes and seascapes have been much admired. It is not surprising when you examine the range of possibilities for pictures on this theme. We originate from our natural surroundings. We have always been dependent on them for our survival and have regarded the changing natural world with reverence, awe and appreciation. There is also a certain nostalgia connected with land and seascapes. The timeless element of scenes, unencumbered by man's blemishes, offers the viewer a glimpse of wholesomeness and constancy. Landscape paintings were once described to me as 'windows on to a world of our own choosing'. This seems such an apt expression, applying in some sense to all paintings, but particularly capturing the essence of land and seascapes.

You need not search long to find a good scene for a landscape. Books and magazines offer plenty of information and the photography and reproduction qualities are excellent. A short car or bus ride to the outskirts of a city should be productive of ideas, too. It is not necessary to travel to distant mountain ranges or areas of great beauty. The intimate corner of a paddock with crumbling cowshed and aged oak tree will do. Parks and rivers, intensively farmed fields, or even a golf course would provide subjects if you investigate their potential fully.

Make an effort to look at some pictures in museums, art galleries and in library books. The appreciation of old master paintings may seem to be the preserve of art historians, but the newcomer can look at and enjoy pictures without having any significant knowledge. Try to understand what special quality the artist was aiming to convey. Do not be afraid to dislike some pictures as much as you like others. Maybe the artist was trying to show you something unpleasant. Above all, see if you can tell which painter had the most joy in making his pictures. It will help you develop your own ability to select an idea for your work, which will inspire you and give pleaure to those who will look at it.

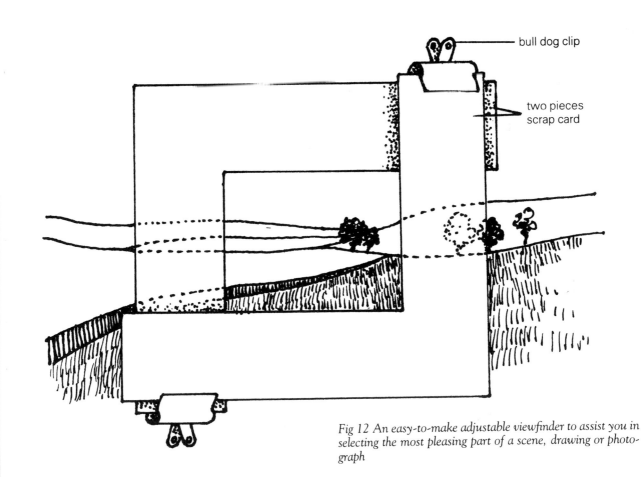

bull dog clip

two pieces scrap card

Fig 12 *An easy-to-make adjustable viewfinder to assist you in selecting the most pleasing part of a scene, drawing or photograph*

'Lacy Daisies': a decorative image which is a development of the watercolour sketch entitled *'Ancient Track'* below

'Ancient Track': a watercolour sketch showing the technique of using a 'wash' in the sky, and combining pencil, paint and brush marks

Fig 13 An ordinary scene can be transformed into an artistic
composition by simply altering the angle from which you view it

Seasons, weather conditions, time of day and carefully chosen viewpoints are all vital to the eventual merits of the picture. An uninteresting or seemingly featureless scene can be transformed into an outstanding image if you observe it skilfully. To illustrate this point, try to remember a time when you noticed something remarkable about your familiar surroundings. Perhaps you were prompted to exclaim that the flowering cherry trees on your regular route to work were unusually laden with blossom one year, or that the morning sunshine was glinting on the river. Maybe the snow had been driven into weird shapes, transforming a normal scene into an icy-blue 'moonscape'. You could be especially fond of sunlight showing through spring green leaves, or of gentle mists or summer heat-haze.

The angle from which you look at your scene can change the whole feeling of the picture. Look carefully while you are walking around and notice how the scene alters as you move. In Fig 13 you can see how the first composition is unremarkable, whereas the second reveals a more dramatic viewpoint, giving the image an eye-catching impact. Always try to select the view which shows the subject off best.

Gardens and Houses
Gardens and houses are often portrayed in paintings. They have an old-world charm similar to that evoked by landscapes. Perhaps they display the sort of tranquillity many of us long for, like the stereotyped 'roses round the door' retirement cottage, or the gentle art of horticulture, which is so popular.

Gardens are full of texture, pattern and colour, superimposed against brick, stone and wood. They are splendid subjects for Thread Paintings since they incorporate the decorative elements of embroidery as well as scope for artistic interpretation.

Contrasts in the appearance of plant forms against the regularity of architecture and garden furniture could be emphasised in your painting. In a composition full of busy shapes and mixed colours, the relief provided by a patch of smoothness is often a helpful device for allowing the eye to rest within the image.

Plants grow in a wonderful array of colours and shapes. By designing with several plant types, you could explore many different themes. You might, for example, be inspired by specific colour ranges and base the work on a group of herbaceous plants in these shades only, set against a back-cloth of leaf greens in light or shadow.

The theme you select could be one of special interest to you, perhaps depicting a family home, or a garden belonging to a relative who is an expert gardener.

If you would like to do a scene demanding very little drawing skill, then you could just show a small portion of the house peeping out from behind the plants. Your view could be a close-up among leaves and blossom, or a more general one showing much of the garden lay-out. It could feature swings, trellis, paths, pools, or pets, insects and birds. There is so much to choose from. You are sure to be able to add ideas of your own to my list. Again, the essence of planning is to pick out some aspect which appeals to you and which you would enjoy conveying to the viewer.

The 'Old Rectory Garden' on p23 is a simple composition to emphasise the glowing reds of the pelargoniums overflowing from the tall plant pot beside the path. The dark background of ivy trailing over the garden wall contrasts starkly with these and the other plants, which are lit from the left. It seemed to me that this corner of a much larger garden was sufficient to give a glimpse of the old-world character of the whole and made a striking image in its own right.

Wildlife
When choosing a subject to paint, another approach is to consider the nature of the medium you are going to use and match it with something suitable. Thread Painting can be used to make dots and flecks, crisp lines and blended colours. You could liken these, for example, with animal fur and bird feathers. In close-up, the textures have much in common. The stitches could be used to great advantage in a wildlife picture.

(page 54)

'The Heron': the background colour was sprayed on, using a plastic hair lacquer bottle and fluid paint. The ripples in the water were made by masking off with a paper strip during spraying, and moving the mask a little to repeat the process. The tree, bird and fish were painted with a brush. There are areas left unstitched and some with carefully controlled sewing, an emphasis being placed on the decorative texturing qualities of Thread Painting

Books with photographs of wild creatures are a considerable help since they capture momentary attitudes and expressions of elusive animals, and they offer you the chance to make your studies at leisure in the comfort of your own home. If you are brave enough to take your sketch book and colours to a zoological garden or aviary, you could make some on-the-spot observations. Spontaneous sketching is commendable because it will give plenty of first-hand information of the subjects you wish to paint. You can interpret the sketches into a final design on the background fabric for a Thread Painting, having had the bonus of creating the picture from start to finish. This extra personal artistic input, gained by making your own notes, avoids the likelihood of being influenced by the opinions of an unknown photographer whose interpretation of the subject is already distilled before you can use it.

I used photographs from several reference books to make the picture entitled 'Heron' on p54, but wished to go further than simply copying any established image. At the time, my family was using a selection of library books about Japanese art for research into another project, and the oriental style seemed to amalgamate easily with my desire to paint a bird in Thread Painting. It enabled me to exaggerate the feathery textures and patterns to greater advantage and to show the technique to best effect. I used the nature books and those about Japan as reference, but developed an entirely new design from the information in both.

Clearly, if you wish to use photographs for their instantaneous recording of ideas, it would be by far the best plan to take your own shots. Cameras are available for even the most inexperienced photographer to use with success. You might take a series of your own pet and amalgamate these into one characteristic pose to paint. My four cats are only ever still when sleeping and I am not good at rapid sketching, so I rely on my camera to capture their playfulness, mischief-making and graceful movements.

(page 55)
'Grandma's Lace': a collection of borrowed treasures makes an unusual still-life group, presenting the challenge of portraying lace, glass, pearl, silk, and enamelled silver, all in Thread Painting. Restricting the colour scheme, and limiting the picture area to a small part of the overall group, has produced a pleasing design

Still-life

Should you prefer a static subject which can be relied on to remain unchanged if you cannot finish it in one session, a still-life may be a good theme. The expression 'still-life' refers to an arrangement of a group of objects which have been brought together in a deliberate composition.

Creativity comes into the painting of a still-life right from the start. It is up to you, the artist, to collect together a group of objects which appeal to you and which in some way belong to a theme. They should enhance each other and interest you enough to paint an enthusiastic rendering of them. You will need to spend time arranging them in the most effective positions, considering their surroundings, too. Make some effort to put them in a good light.

Your still-life is not necessarily just a collection of imposing objects, but it can express a meaningful sentiment. If you were to paint a carefully selected group of market produce, it might merely be a faithful portrait of tomatoes, oranges, onions, apples, and so on. However, if you were to show the same articles as they have been dumped on the kitchen table, falling from the shopping-bag at random, they might convey that supermarket-weary moment between arriving home and finding the energy to unpack the groceries into their household order.

The still-life 'Ricky Bear and Friends' on p59 came about as a result of an inspirational little drawing that my daughter had made of a cluster of favourite toys on her own bed, and which included two of our cats who had curled themselves up for an illicit snooze among the toys. The furry toys and the hand-knitted patchwork bedspread clearly lent themselves to Thread Painting, and, although the cats could not be persuaded to regroup themselves for my picture, I was able to make a rendering of the teddies and doll. The result pleased me since the toys are quite recognisable, and the group seems to have that uncanny lifelike quality attributed in nursery stories to toys which come to life behind the young master's back. I suspect that Ricky Bear and his friends are holding a committee meeting about a very serious matter. They certainly look rather earnest.

Traditional still-life subjects include arrangements of flowers, bowls of fruit, bread, cheese, wine bottles, and so on. You could add some suggestions of your own. The equipment relating to a hobby such as fly-fishing, knitting, lacemaking, woodwork or a sport, all have possibilities. You could add a netted fish to the tackle, a partly made jersey to the wool and needles. Such pictures would have a personal touch and might make good birthday presents or special presentations. Always select objects with a reason. The resulting pictures will be more meaningful and probably full of fun, too.

Abstract

Works of art in the twentieth century have taken hitherto unexplored forms, breaking with convention. Artists have become increasingly interested in experimentation, devoting their energies to the qualities in the subject matter and the effectiveness of painting techniques. It is, for example, acceptable to make a picture which simply expresses the artist's enthusiasm for thick, rich patches of paint. He may be inspired by making clashing coloured shapes appear to jump about on the canvas as an optical illusion. Whatever the resulting artistic product, no matter how simple, it is likely that it was arrived at through a series of studies. It is always necessary to have a starting point and to develop the idea through stages to its final design.

If purely representational pictures are not to your taste, you might like to attempt an abstract work. In order to provide yourself with an initial idea, you should spend some time looking around in just the same way as for a realistic picture source. Your range of observation can take in any sphere of knowledge or activity. Working from photographs, sketched notes, tracings, or from the original object, your aim should be to interpret some of the characteristics of that theme without painting a literal portrait of it.

You may need to go through several stages in the development of such a design, all the time embellishing, accentuating and reinterpreting your ideas until you arrive at a personal statement. This final stage may even be so far removed from the original source that it bears no resemblance. Compare this process to the changes wrought to a piece of neighbourhood gossip as it is passed from person to person. Only the salient points are retained, but even these can become exaggerated out of all proportion until they exhibit little of the original fact.

Natural forms such as pieces of lichen-encrusted tree bark, pearly sea-shells, coral formations and fossils are good sources of inspiration. Microscopic studies of tiny creatures, plants and crystalline forms also open up a whole spectrum of possibilities, since unexpectedly beautiful phenomena are often revealed at high magnification. At the opposite end of the scale, examine scientific photographs of space study or geological surveys. Sporting and leisure activities can also provide pleasing images to work on. It does not really matter how you begin, so long as you can find exciting material to develop into a picture.

The watercolour sketch on p50 shows the result of my painting an actual view, using colours as well as initial light pencil notes. This study became a distillation of the visual evidence. Naturally, one cannot be expected to make a photographic record of the scene. It follows that the sketching process is in itself an abstraction of reality.

'Lacy Daisies' illustrated on p51 is one more stage further removed from the reality of that same cart track and field margin in my sketch. It is simply based on the colour theme, plus the general composition, and exaggerates them. The picture, however, has not lost all of its original representational qualities and can still be interpreted as a field edge with distant trees.

This chapter covers only a fraction of the potential spheres of study which could inspire your Thread Painting. Since any art form is founded on the input of individual ideas, you, the reader, will be able to contribute a great deal more to this limited collection of suggestions.

It would be easy for the beginner to take the task of picture-making too seriously, to read too avidly, to listen to all sorts of tips, rules and recommendations, and then to become bowed down with the seeming complexities of the process. The best advice is to follow your own beliefs. Many great artists have done just that. Seek help, read and go to classes only when you need to reinforce your learning. The important thing is to start picture-making as soon as you can. It will teach you much more quickly.

'Ricky Bear and Friends'

'Aldeborough Beach': the main features in this composition are clear and separate. The sky is entirely paint, giving a smooth background upon which to superimpose the narrow band of precise detail of the fishing boats. The highly banked shingle beach was painted and worked in thread with special attention paid to its contours and to the decreasing size of pebble texture into the distance. Some details on the boats were made more accurately by adjusting the sewing-machine to a normal satin stitch setting, with feed teeth engaged and an embroidery foot attached

6
COMPOSITION

Composition is a fundamental part of picture planning. It entails the organisation of all the elements in your image into the most satisfactory design.

The surface of a picture is flat, but the artist often wishes to give the viewer a feeling of three dimensions, of space, movement and mood. Careful arrangements of these parts of the picture can produce some convincing effects and can transform a hitherto unspectacular subject into a work of art.

There are some rules for composition which have been fashionable with artists. These depend largely on custom and have only noticeably changed when influenced by society. Some of these rules are still familiar to us. In addition, a more liberal approach has become acceptable, wherein artists have taken their work beyond restrictive traditions to explore composition anew. Innovation now goes hand in hand with convention.

When you are designing your picture, you need to bear the following points in mind and gradually you will become accustomed to doing them naturally. Painting as a whole is an intuitive subject. Like so many activities, it becomes complicated when it is analysed and discussed. Do not expect to read and digest all the information offered, but come back to it from time to time to consolidate your experience.

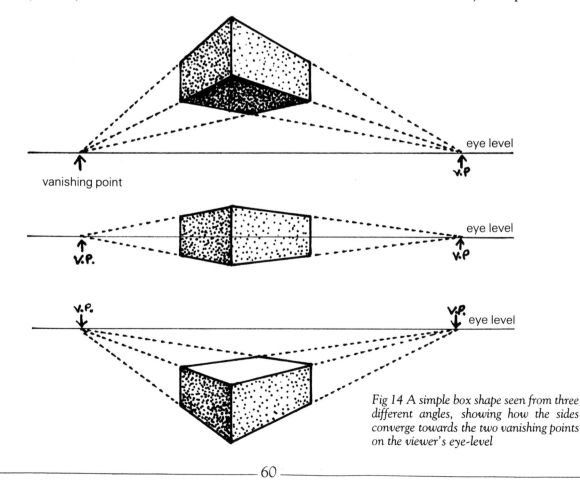

Fig 14 A simple box shape seen from three different angles, showing how the sides converge towards the two vanishing points on the viewer's eye-level

PERSPECTIVE

One of the conventions by which artists express realism in their paintings is the formula we call perspective. The use of perspective drawing gives the viewer the impression of depth and distance, making a flat picture surface look like a three-dimensional scene. These rules are based on the principle that objects appear to the human eye to get smaller at a regular rate as they recede from the onlooker. There are some drawbacks to following these rules too closely because they rely on the artist keeping his viewing direction static and portraying his scene like the single optical view of a camera. Many artists have searched for better ways of showing three dimensions, but the majority of us can best understand the approach to perspective described here, and it is widely used.

As it is a visual topic, the subject of perspective is easier to comprehend using diagrams in conjunction with explanation (see Fig 14). In perspective, all vertical and horizontal lines remain at the same angle, but appear shorter the further away they are from the viewer. All other lines which are parallel with each other in life, but which recede from the viewer, will seem to converge towards the distance, until they meet at a vanishing point on the horizon (see Fig 15). In the street scene, the house sides, road, trees and fence are all parallel, and recede to the same vanishing point. Drawing perspective can become complicated by the introduction of several vanishing points – even a simple cube can have two. If you are interested in this topic, it may prove useful to read further books about it and to practise more thoroughly.

A convincing exercise for the beginner is to tape a piece of clear plastic to a window, or to stand some glass or Perspex safely in front of a suitable subject, such as a street scene, and then to draw simple outlines of what is seen. Trace them on to the clear material with a felt pen or wax marker. Do remember

Fig 15 In this view, the row of houses, trees and fence are all parallel with the road, and they recede towards the same vanishing point on the horizon, while the verticals remain upright, but shorter and closer as they recede

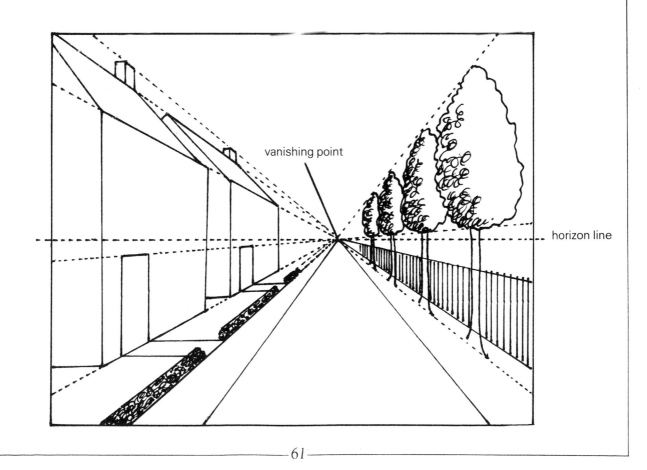

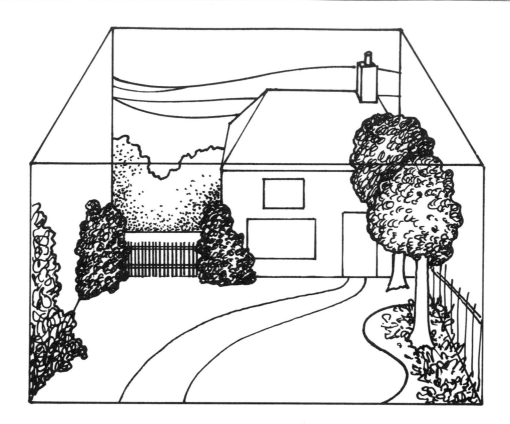

Fig 16 *All the features of your picture occupy a specific position within the picture space, like a stage lay-out (as in drawing 1), and can be rearranged to best effect so that, when viewed from the front (as in drawing 2), they make a pleasing and meaningful picture*

to keep your head in one position as far as possible. Moving from side to side or up and down will alter your view and confuse your drawing. An easier alternative to this, although less convincing, would be to use tracing paper over a photograph of buildings, rail tracks, or roads, particularly if the view shows these receding into the distance.

Space between objects can also be shown by careful recording of the changes which occur in the apparent colour of objects as they recede from the onlooker. This is called atmospheric perspective (see p37).

You can see the phenomenon of perspective as you travel about. Try this test for yourself. Experience tells you that an adult can be expected to be a predictable size as can a car or a house. Ask a friend to stand beside you. Note how tall he or she is. Now ask your friend to walk at normal speed away from you down a path. Hold out your hand at full length, with your thumb in the air. Close one eye to reduce your width of vision. Call to the friend to stop when your thumb seems to obscure him completely. He is unlikely to have walked very far into the distance, but is already small in your perception.

SPACE

Most pictures deal with the spatial arrangement of items within an image. To explain this, think of the elements in your picture as the contents of a stage set, with props and actors included. Imagine that a piece of glass is lowered in place of the curtain and that it is the actual picture plane or canvas upon which you are going to paint. All the parts can be moved about under your directorship. They could be placed next to, or in front of each other, in rows or spaced apart at your will.

The most satisfactory view will be for all the elements to be so arranged that the onlooker can believe in the scene and can understand the artist's intentions. He will not have his view unnecessarily obscured and he will also find carefully grouped details and space in which to rest the eye. He may notice a focal point to attract his attention, just as he would be drawn to the leading actor in a play.

LEADING THE EYE

All compositions, whether realistic or abstract, need to hold the viewer's attention by leading the

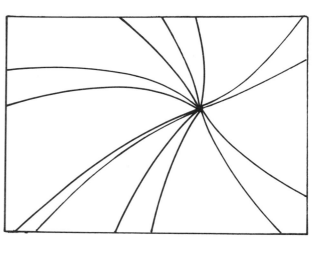

Fig 17 Focal points: a picture often needs a feature which attracts the eye, inviting the viewer into the space within and holding his attention

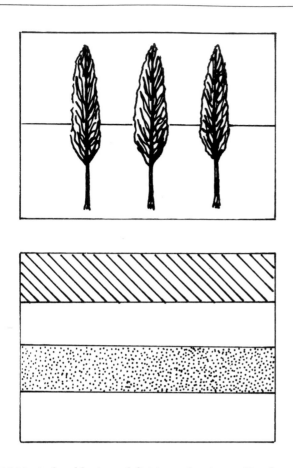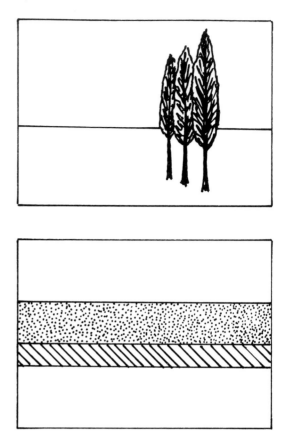

Fig 18 Vertical and horizontal divisions of a picture. Regular spacing may be employed, but the irregular grouping of similar features can be much more pleasing to the eye

creates a dual choice between two picture areas, with weakened attraction.

It is best to vary the proportions within your picture space.

CONTRASTS AND VARIETY

In composition, neighbouring areas of similar appearance may not complement each other and, in fact, could lessen their individual qualities. Smooth areas will be shown off to best advantage in contrast with texture. Light contrasts shade, red enhances green, lines complement dots, and so on. You should aim to use all the features in your picture to their best potential.

A painting which is totally full of detailed work may be as off-putting to the viewer as to eat an extravagant meal cooked with lashings of cream and brandy, but with no simple courses or flavours to clear the palate. Similarly, an image entirely in bold, bright colour may have the same effect as a whole symphony played fortissimo. To appreciate the finer qualities in any work of art, there should be variety.

eye into the canvas and by a well-balanced arrangement within its boundaries. In simple terms, a picture featuring a winding path leading from foreground to distance is likely to catch the eye, offering an invitation to explore the scene. A road coming in at one side, going straight across and out the other is less welcoming.

The same sense of visual confusion could be created by placing a tall tree in the centre, dividing the picture space into two unrelated halves, whereas placing the same tree to one side opens up a larger space. These irregular proportions are more pleasing.

You should consider that your picture will allow people to enter the scene, in their imagination, and partake of the sights and feelings you are showing them. That misplaced road could invite them in and usher them out again as if it were leading somewhere better without stopping. That tall central tree only

7
FROM DESIGN TO FABRIC

Once the idea for your image is at a suitable stage to translate into Thread Painting, you will need to copy it out on the fabric background. There are several ways which might appeal to you, depending on your degree of confidence and upon the type of source material you are working from.

TRACING

If you have chosen to begin by copying a simple picture directly from a magazine or book, and the original is the same size as your proposed Thread Painting, then you could draw the outline, using tracing paper or household greaseproof paper (if that is transparent enough for you).

Using carbon paper between the tracing and your fabric, or by following the manufacturer's instructions for haberdasher's transfer pencil, retrace your lines so that they are repeated on the fabric. The outlines will form a foundation for your painting stage. You are free to follow the original accurately, or to alter and develop the themes to suit your own purpose. The painting and stitching stages provide you with a dual opportunity to add individuality to the work. Do not forget that you will reverse the image if you turn the tracing over.

GRID SYSTEM

If tracing proves to be too mechanical a method of transferring your idea to the work, you could employ a procedure which relies on guidance and estimation, such as a grid reference system which will assist you in marking out the design, but which allows freedom to make changes as you go along.

You can make a simple grid by drawing in waterproof pen on to a clear plastic or acetate sheet. Another durable method is to make a cardboard window and stretch some black thread across it, taping the ends to the card (see Fig 19). It should be

accurately measured and have a vertical and horizontal thread crossing in the middle.

A grid is a most useful piece of equipment. It can be helpful in selecting the best part of the image, in copying designs, and in enlarging or reducing them. This is how it works:

1 Lay your grid over the design. Imagining that the squares are panes of glass in a window and that you can pull blinds down or across, decide which squares to leave uncovered. Masking off unwanted areas will help. Select a pleasing composition.

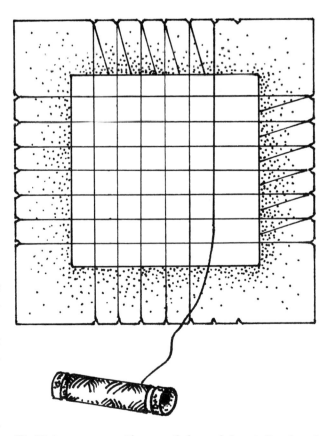

Fig 19 A permanent grid can easily be made by winding thread around a notched window of card

'After the Snowfall': winter scenes are popular subjects for many artists. They are often too cold to inspire me, but this is an exception. The sunshine made beautiful colours in the snow. The warmth in the sunlight and wonderful lacy patterns formed by the trees against the sky tempted me to record the scene

'After Vincent Van Gogh': one of the members of the Post Impressionist group of painters was Vincent Van Gogh, whose work was stronger in colour and emphatic in texture. His pictures can seem at first glance to be over-rich and busy.

However, I find them tremendously exciting, especially when looking at the originals in an art gallery.

This Thread Painting was done in an attempt to explore the incredible intensity common in his work, and because the technique of Thread Painting offered me a chance to use blobs and dashes of colour in the same way.

The subject was a view of some cottages near my home. They showed some of the features I was looking for to adapt to Van Gogh's style. The English landscape seldom looks as colourful and crisp as southern France where he worked, so I had to freely interpret the natural colours by reference to reproductions of his pictures. Making this picture was most enjoyable.

grid overlay

Fig 20 The small picture can be copied and even enlarged, using a grid reference system. Mark out the main elements of the original on to your work, placing them as accurately as possible according to their 'grid reference' position

2 On the background fabric, mark the outside edges of your intended picture. Do not work too close to the embroidery hoop. Make sure that the shape of your picture is similar to the original, even if it is bigger or smaller in proportion.

3 Next, you can mark out very lightly (it will have to be covered up with paint later) a simple grid in pencil on your fabric, to match the number of squares filled by the original. Try to include a middle vertical and horizontal line.

4 You can now compare the position of the most important features in your design with the corresponding places on the fabric and mark them in. Start with any obvious divisions of the space, eg the horizon line, or the most prominent verticals. Draw in as much as you can using the grid overlay as a map reference guide, by working out the coordinates.

5 Remove the grid. Sketch in any further useful detail and paint it in, still looking back at the original, copying the information you need and perhaps developing the theme to your satisfaction.

6 This grid overlay system can be used to enlarge or decrease a design retaining its proportion. Simply

light pencil marks

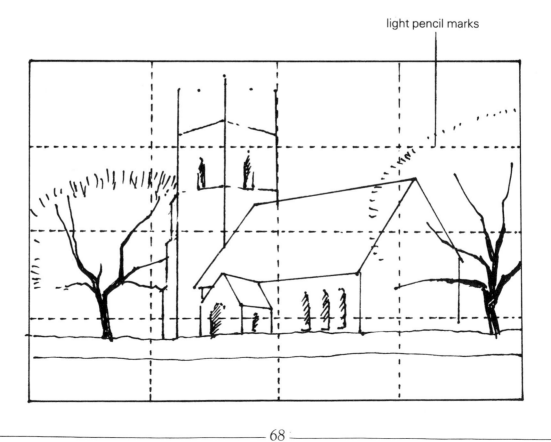

compare the positions of all essential parts of the original with their reference location and draw them in, larger or smaller as necessary to suit the scale you are using.

Eventually, you will be able to dispense with the grid and make reasonable judgements about positioning by your own estimation.

Total accuracy is not necessary in copying a picture. The sooner you add touches of your own, the better. Aim to be more than just a copyist. You are sure to have the most pleasure from achieving your very own designs, especially when they are admired by others.

Sketching

Preliminary drawings and colour notes on paper may form the transition stages between the source idea and the final design. Working from pen, pencil or paint sketches is a way of gathering together snippets of information which can be amalgamated into a final satisfactory image for a Thread Painting.

Use sketches for two purposes. First, they will make you look and learn about your chosen subject matter. The activity of drawing or painting exploratory notes will require you to examine thoroughly what you see in order to record it accurately on paper. Secondly, sketching begins the interpretative process, wherein the artist gives his personal version of reality. Even the most thorough drawing must be selective. The artist omits details of minor value, and immediately emphasises that which appeals to him. A series of sketches, possibly in different media, provides a collective impression of the subject from which the artist can evolve a final work.

Development of ideas through sketching may well be suitable for you even if you are a beginner. It will help you plan a picture thoughtfully before rushing into a finished piece. Also, if you are competent at sketching, it will be no problem to mark out your final composition on to the fabric, without relying on any of the mechanical methods.

Direct Painting

Thread Painting is a technique which allows the freedom to work spontaneously because of the sewing-machine's rapid output. It matches your mood since you can respond to moments of inspiration with vivacious stitching or deliberate precision.

Taking into account the directness of the medium, it would be particularly suitable to work your idea straight on to the fabric from the source. This is a sensible approach for those who are inclined to overwork their drawings, thus losing some of the original inspiration.

Direct painting may involve taking your colouring set and stretched fabric to an outdoor location and working on it straight from your chosen view. This directness will give you some valuable advantages. Drawings and photographs only contain a limited amount of information. They cannot bring you the full range of experience which your senses could absorb on site.

The more directly you translate your perception of that reality into the finished work, the greater your chances of producing a fully expressive picture. It is likely to reflect the subject matter with the authority of a first-hand report, and also convey your personal interpretation and emotional responses.

An added advantage of this approach, especially if carried out in the open air, is that your colours will be fresher and your brushwork livelier than if you were tempted to sit at these preparatory stages too long in the comfort of home. Uninterrupted daylight and the sense of immediacy felt outdoors, should bring out honest, well-observed qualities in your painting and will help to carry those initial feelings through to the finished picture.

Abstract Approach

Bearing in mind those comparisons between the characteristics of Thread Painting and of direct methods of applying your chosen image, it would be rewarding to explore other ways to make a spontaneous theme.

If you are an obsessive doodler, you might put your intuitive talent to good use. With a pen, pencil, felt marker or brush, you can doodle directly on to a fabric which is coloured, plain or even self-patterned. Consider colour schemes as part of the design.

To go a stage further, you might doodle several sample pieces on paper, select the most promising pattern, and have it enlarged or reduced on a photocopier. Then part, or all of it, may be traced on to the work.

'Water Garden': an unconventional view of a decorative and popular subject

Alternatively, a purely abstract design or simple pictorial composition can be put on to fabric, using torn or cut paper as templates. It is wise to draw the outside edges of your picture before assembling paper pieces in a pleasing order so that they can be considered within the given space. This kind of design relies heavily on the factors relating to good composition, as discussed in Chapter 6, since there are few representational elements to make the work attractive.

There are yet other possibilities for random image making. They loosely fall into the category of 'action painting'. Sponges, string, and so on can be dipped into paint and printed on the background. You might make potato cuts. You could sprinkle, dab or trail paint. The process may not be totally random, as control can still be exercised over the arrangement of patterns.

Try spraying on a liquid paint or dye, producing a kind of air-brushed effect. By combining torn paper shapes and spray you could develop an exciting abstract featuring crisp or ragged edges and gentle diffused sprayed colour.

In keeping with the whole process of Thread Painting, the early stages are open to your full range of inventiveness.

Fig 21 Making a design on fabric using torn or cut paper mask, and spray-on colour. The paper shape can be moved, or substituted for another, and the spraying repeated

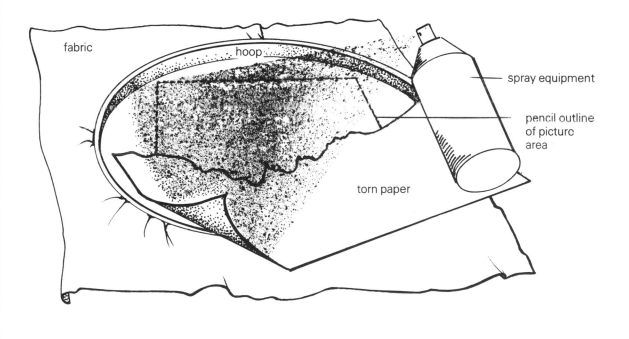

fabric

hoop

spray equipment

pencil outline of picture area

torn paper

8

PRESENTATION

It is my firm belief that a piece of art work, which has evolved through all the stages of planning, effort and creativity, and which has given you pleasure in the making, deserves finishing touches that will do it proper justice.

Extra time and expenditure in attending to the presentation of a Thread Painting often enhances the work to a remarkable degree. Your choice of finishing materials depends largely on the intent and likely destination of your work. Many Thread Paintings will certainly be finished as pictures for display in the home. Therefore, the most useful advice will be about types of mounting and framing. Resourceful readers may want to try the medium with other purposes in mind, and some suggestions are included here.

STRETCHING THE WORK

Finished pictures, when taken off an embroidery hoop, tend to distort and buckle because of the accumulated tension caused by so much stitching. The first step is to restore the fabric to its flat state. You will need to stretch it permanently over a piece of card to make it taut.

1 Choose card which is firm but slightly flexible and cut it to a size just a little larger than the image itself. Very large pictures may need to be stretched on hardboard.
2 Put your picture face down on a clean table-top. Place the card over the reverse side of the picture.
3 Thread a needle with sewing thread (a stronger one for large pictures). Do not cut a length, but leave it to unwind on demand from the spool.
4 Fold the sides of the fabric over your card and stitch backwards and forwards across the gap in a lacing movement. The result should look like harp strings linking the two edges across the card.
5 When you have reached the end, cut the thread

from the spool and secure it at the point where you began. Leave your needle threaded up to finish off later.
6 Lift the work and flex the card a little. This will slacken the lacing and allow you to pull the threads tighter. Go on tightening gently until you are sure that the work will be taut when the work is pressed flat again.
7 Finish off the needle end securely, ensuring that the lacing is still tight. Flatten out the card.
8 Turn the work around and repeat the lacing process so that the picture is stretched side to side and top to bottom.

If your picture is circular or oval, but is to be displayed in a rectangular frame, you can stretch it on to a square piece of card by the same process. For curved images that are intended for a round or oval frame, the card stretching process will have to follow the outline of the image and be laced up like the spokes in a wheel. This is much more difficult and it is advisable to take really prized pieces to a professional framer.

Always try to stretch your Thread Painting where its use allows – it will look so much better. Do avoid the use of glue to complete the process because so many adhesives deteriorate with age and could spoil your work.

Avoid dampening the work to get it flat. You may have used paints or dyes that would run and spoil your picture. Try not to resort to pressing the work with an iron. This only flattens out the texture which you have so painstakingly achieved.

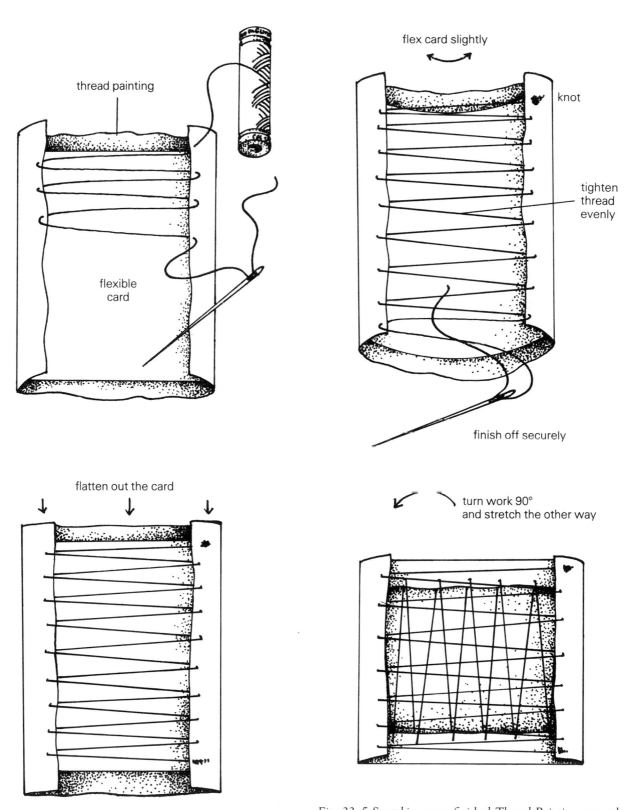

thread painting

flexible card

flex card slightly

knot

tighten thread evenly

finish off securely

flatten out the card

turn work 90° and stretch the other way

Figs 22–5 Stretching your finished Thread Painting on card without the need to dampen the cloth

'Impression of a Frosty Morning': Claude Monet was a foremost member of the French Impressionists and his work has always inspired me. Having looked at many reproductions of his paintings, I attempted to emulate his style in this little picture of a Norfolk field in winter. It shows a morning on which the frost was still extremely hard and the rime clung to every twig, making candy floss trees. Everywhere was extraordinarily still. Although the landscape was blanketed in white, there appeared to be magical colours all around.

I have used warm colours in the sunlight and cold crisp blues in the shadow. The picture has a simple composition with very little detail and relies heavily on colour effects

MOUNTING THE PICTURE

There is a temptation to regard these last stages as purely mechanical and unrelated to the creative input which goes before. Both the mount and the frame can actually improve the image if chosen with care. They should be undertaken as part of the overall plan. There is even the possibility of using this stage as a chance to extend the theme of your picture.

You should choose a suitably coloured mount board by taking your work to the stockist who offers a wide selection. Match colours in daylight, if possible. Ask the assistant to allow you to select by a window. Colours can look quite different in artificial light, so think of that too. Seek the advice of the retailer if you need help. Choose a frame at the same time so that you have an idea of the final effect.

Double mounts are often worth considering. You can pick two colours which match the picture, perhaps a light and a dark tone for variety. The outer mount might be a different shape. These are simple devices for making a pleasant surround, giving the whole some restful space between picture and the final boundary of the frame.

Most often, the neater, simpler mounts and frames are best. However, it may improve the overall design to test out one of the following suggestions:

1 Use contrasting textured mounts, such as linen-look, marbled paper or fabric-covered card.
2 Alter the mount in some way. Try binding it with coloured threads, tapes and ribbons. Alternatively, you might paint on the surface. The pattern could be simple lines, dots and doodles, or a continuation of the picture theme outwards to the frame.
3 Perhaps the aperture in the mount could be cut in such a way as to echo the picture theme. It may even become part of it, as, for example, an archway around a rose garden.

As you can see, the scope is enormous. It is worthwhile planning your whole project from the initial stages onward with a special mount and frame style in mind. Pre-planning helps to maintain a unified approach.

Cutting the Mount

Use a good knife, such as a craft tool or surgical scalpel. Renew the blade whenever it gets the slightest bit blunt because the cut must always be clean and precise. Damaged blades make ragged edges and, of course, are harder to cut with. Work on top of an old piece of board, card or professional cutting-mat so as not to scratch the work-table. Gather together all the tools you need and have them within easy reach. Always keep your hands clean and free from grease. Mount board will mark at the slightest touch of hot or dirty fingers, and this cannot be put right. If you have naturally moist fingers, handle the mounts by the edges and cover the good surface with a spare piece of paper while you work.

To cut the mount, follow this procedure:

1 Measure the space in the picture frame, including the rebate, and cut your mount board to fit into it as exactly as you can. Always make sure that the corners are right angles (90°).
2 Measure exactly the size of your Thread Painting image.
3 Calculate the width of mount border surrounding the picture as follows:
   Subtract the image width from the total width of the card you have cut. Here is an example: total card width 20cm (8in), minus image width 12cm (5in) equals 8cm (3in).
   Halve this remainder; in my example, the border width each side of the image will therefore be 4cm (1½in).
   Measure similarly to calculate the top and bottom borders.
4 On the *right side* of the card, mark lightly in soft pencil small dots, measuring out the border width from the outside edge. Measure accurately.
5 Do the same for the top and bottom borders. Lightly pencil in lines between the dots to show where you will cut the aperture. Allow the pencil lines to cross over at the corners. Any pencil marks on the front of the card will have to be gently erased later. It is wise to mark very lightly, using a soft leaded pencil (2B, 4B or 6B), so as to avoid any indentation in the card surface.
6 Hold your straight edge firmly along one of the lines and cut from point to point exactly on the markings. Do not let your knife run on beyond

the cross-over points which denote the corners of the aperture.

7 Cut all four sides in the same manner. The waste card will fall out of the middle, leaving a window for the image.

8 Tape your Thread Painting in its correct position behind the mount.

9 Cut any second mount by the same process, altering the measurements to suit your requirements.

10 Sandwich your mounted picture between glass (if you wish to protect it) and another sheet of board, ready to slip it into a frame. Secure the work in its frame by the recommended method. Some frames are made of wood and are suitable for holding the picture in place with pins or tacks. Professional framers have a kind of staple

gun which clips small metal wedges into the wood. Plastic and aluminium frames have special devices for holding the picture. There are many variations.

The size and proportion of border around your picture is a matter of taste. My work is almost always mounted with equal-sized borders at the sides and top and bottom. Conventionally, it is said to be correct to have a slightly deeper border at the bottom. You should consider how either approach will look on your image.

A professional framer may cut the apertures in the card at an angle to give them a bevelled appearance. Again, this is optional. A straight cut can look as good and is much easier to do at home.

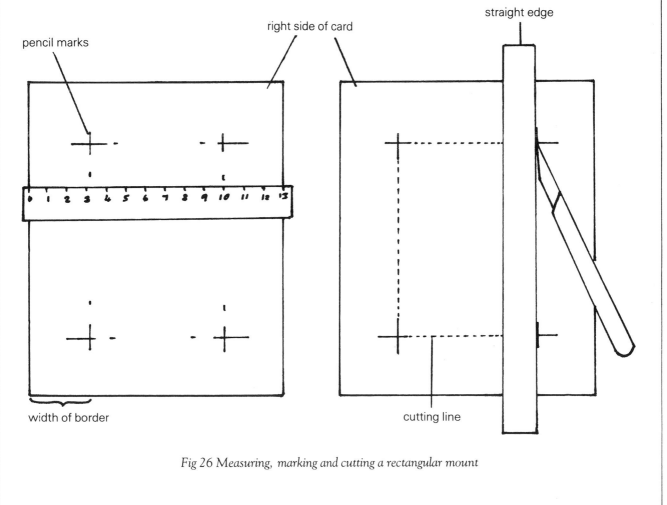

Fig 26 Measuring, marking and cutting a rectangular mount

'Two Oaks': there are particular times in a year and also certain views which especially appeal to me. Here is a combination of both. There is a brief moment when the wheat fields are beginning to produce heads of grain, but before they ripen, when the landscape is soft and beautiful, all in gentle greens.

I often paint pictures from an opening to a field, where the farm vehicles have made interesting ruts in the ground and where the wild plants flourish. This picture is of an almost incidental glimpse into a field and features two lovely oaks

Circular Mounts

This will involve a steady hand since you will be drawing free-hand around a circle. Special circular mount cutters are usually expensive pieces of equipment. While they are, of course, the most accurate means of making a good circle, it is quite possible to succeed by hand.

If a free-hand circle seems to be too demanding a task, try to find a plate the right size. You will need to find a way of keeping it central on the mount, while cutting around it as a template.

1 Cut your card to the right size for the frame.

2 Mark the centre of the card with a cross by taking a diagonal line with your ruler, from corner to corner, and then from opposite corners. The lines will meet exactly in the middle, provided the card is really square.

3 With a pair of compasses, estimate the size of circle your picture will require. Place the compass point near the centre of your Thread Painting. Open the compasses as wide as you can and turn them without marking your work. Adjust the radius until you are satisfied that the circle they will draw is the correct size for the image.

4 Keeping the compasses open at that radius, place the point firmly into the centre of the mount card and draw a clear accurate circle on the *front* of the card.

5 Take a sharp knife. Slowly and gently, score a first incision around the circle. Cutting free-hand around a pencil line takes some practice. When you have gone around once, making a slight cut in the card, it is easier to go around again, scoring deeper each time until the waste card drops out of the middle, leaving the circular aperture.

6 See stage 8 onwards, p77.

Oval Mounts

Oval shapes vary in proportion considerably because they are based on a width and length calculation. The easiest way of dealing with oval mounts is to look for a suitable template and use it to cut around. Ready-cut mounts are available from most framing shops. You could buy your ovals for each picture or keep one as a template.

Fig 28 shows you a method of drawing an ellipse to your own measurements to use for a template. It is somewhat inaccurate but will certainly produce a good enough oval for mount cutting.

1 Decide how long and how wide the oval must be at its maximum.

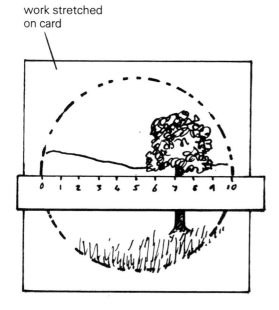

work stretched on card

Fig 27 Mounting a circular picture in a square surround

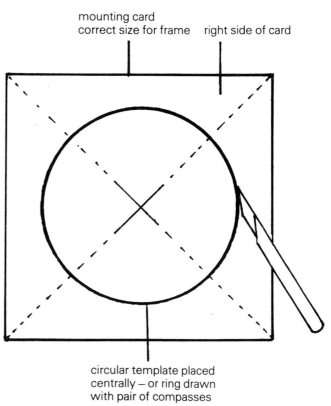

mounting card correct size for frame   right side of card

circular template placed centrally — or ring drawn with pair of compasses

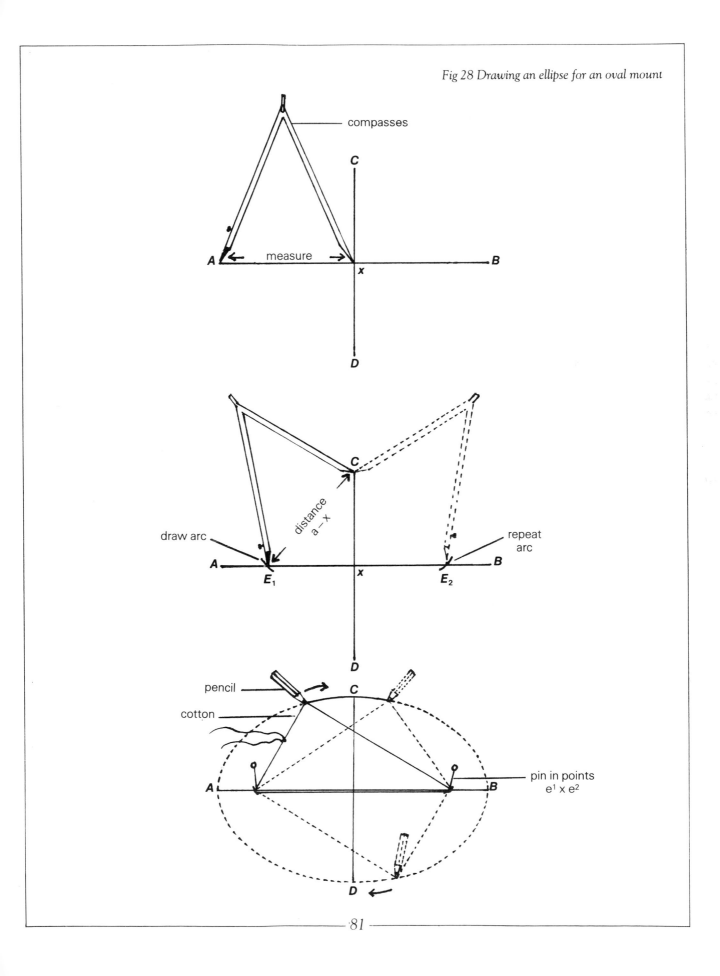

Fig 28 *Drawing an ellipse for an oval mount*

compasses

C

A ← measure → B

x

D

distance
a – x

draw arc

C

A B

E₁ x E₂

repeat
arc

D

pencil

cotton

C

A B

pin in points
e¹ x e²

D

2 Work on a thick piece of card. Rule a line the length of the longest axis AB, then rule another at 90° to it, making it the length of the width axis CD. They should intersect in the middle.

3 With a pair of compasses, opened out to a radius measuring A to X, place the compass point at C and drawn an arc at E_1 and E_2).

4 Stick two map pins firmly into points E_1 and E_2 and another in point C.

5 Tie a piece of non-elastic thread to form a triangle around the three pins.

6 Remove pin C. Replace it with a finely sharpened pencil. Keeping the thread triangle taut, draw the outline of your oval, using point D instead of C for the second side.

7 Cut it out carefully, with a sharp knife, to use as a template.

If you have already decided where your picture will hang, its surroundings might influence the choice of mount and frame to some degree. Your colours and framing style can help the picture belong to the room.

FRAMING

Choosing a frame is just as important as mounting your work. In Chapter 6 on composition my advice was to avoid over-elaborate or too standard a grouping of the pictorial elements. This also applies to the presentation in that it should complement your work, rather than overpower it or merely repeat the theme. A very ornate frame might be excessive around a heavily encrusted picture. Your choice should really do the job of completing the picture without being obtrusive. If in doubt about getting the balance right, ask other people to give their opinions.

There are many types of frame available commercially. Some are sold ready made up, others come in kit form, and also you can have lengths specially cut for you to make up at home or for the professional to assemble for you. The corners are usually mitred, that is, cut at 45° angles so that they join neatly.

Look for the right visual appearance when choosing, but also bear in mind that the sandwich of glass, mount, picture and backing board could be quite thick, and so you may need a frame with a fairly deep rebate.

Some less conventional alternatives may be worth considering. You might be lucky enough to find inexpensive but serviceable frames in a second-hand shop. You could repolish or repaint them to your liking.

If there is a keen woodworker in the family, you could design a combined work of art, using a pur-

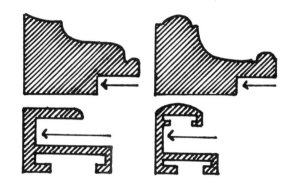

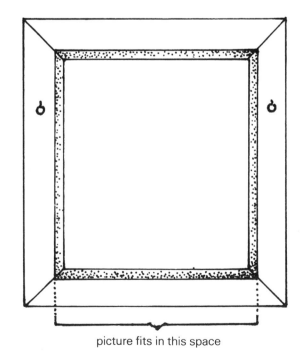

picture fits in this space

Fig 29 Picture frames have a space designed to hold the image, plus glass, mount-board and backing board

'Late Autumn Sunshine': the luminosity of sunlight, as it penetrates the mist, emphasises the sense of space and mood in this picture. Detail becomes increasingly distinct towards the foreground. The interplay of light and shade enhances the dramatic effect

pose-made frame. It need not follow a normal shape. Perhaps a triangular frame would suit an eye-catching abstract painting, or the frame could be in the shape of a window, with the Thread Painting as the view through. The facility to carry out a whole project as a family is a splendid opportunity for team work and might even involve the children.

A frame need only be the boundary between the fiction of the picture and its real surroundings. You might even use unconventional materials, such as card bound with cord, or resin moulding kits. Box frames, where the surround stands proud of the work, are useful when the picture is heavily textured and needs to be kept uncrushed by glass. One can also buy metal or plastic clips which hold the glass/picture/backing-board sandwich in place without the need for a frame at all. Some styles of painting suit this approach particularly well.

There is a choice between framing your work without glass, using clear glass or the non-reflecting variety. Some people feel that glass forms a barrier between viewer and picture, while others prefer to cover the work for protection. Certainly, it is more pleasant to have an uninterrupted view, but atmospheric pollution of all kinds is very destructive to textiles and it is preferable that one's pictures stand a good chance of surviving as long as possible. Non-reflecting types of glass can be used, but they do tend to make fine detail less well defined and are best used on large-scale, bold paintings.

9

MAKING THE MOST OF THREAD PAINTING

The term Thread Painting implies a pictorial bias. The enthusiasm which I feel for the technique owes much to the widening scope brought about by the development of a hitherto embroidery-based process into a fully fledged painting medium. It dispels any preconceived notion that art is in some way in a higher league than craft. By allowing the emphasis to be placed on any aspect of the creative process, be it craftsmanship, decorative expertise, manual dexterity, design skills or painterly qualities, it fulfils beyond the limitations of many other media.

This book concentrates on the direct and most obvious uses for Thread Painting in the belief that thorough familiarity of the medium will enable anyone to adapt it to maximum effect within their own creative repertoire. Since its main feature clearly owes a great deal to embroidery, it is reasonable to expect many readers to use it as an addition to their store of stitchery skills. Thread Painting may even be an extension of the embroiderer's picture-making ambition, or it could be most useful in texturing and surface decoration. The colour-blending qualities also have a place in embroidery.

To explore the subject of embroidery here would be superfluous to the main purpose. The embroiderer will know instinctively which stitch to use, how to make it and what effect is likely to be achieved. Thread Painting is most emphatically not a means of mechanically copying any of these skills. It represents a new range of effects which ought to be used to good purpose. There is a strong possibility that much more still can be made of the medium, given the inventiveness and diversity of creative minds. Consider, for instance, some of the qualities already apparent in the technique.

LINEAR EFFECTS

With the sewing-machine set for running stitch, one can achieve drawn lines similar to those done with pen and ink. If you examine a detailed pen drawing you can see how descriptive the lines are. They can delineate outlines, follow three-dimensional form and texture. By hatching and cross-hatching, or spotting, an artist can reproduce the way light and shade appear to express shapes. Lines are an integral part of doodling and pattern-making.

In hand embroidery there are also stitches which can be used in a linear way. In combination, bearing in mind the limitations of each, you could make a fascinating drawing.

RANDOM STITCHES

Thread Painting seldom exhibits tidy stitchery. Unless you are highly skilled with a sewing-machine, most of your threads will be somewhat randomly applied. In response to excitement or inspiration, some of the sewing will even appear wildly and casually done. In stark contrast, most hand embroidery is a slower, more deliberate process, and no matter how rapidly you work, the technique limits the degree of spontaneity you can achieve. These two qualities, so opposite in nature, might go well together in one work. Imagine, for example, a picture of a ship tossed in an ocean storm. The ship might be portrayed in appliquéd pieces of smooth fabric for sails and planking, the rigging made of couched threads and details in a variety of neatly worked hand stitches. The storm with its violent seas, spray and howling winds could be best expressed in Thread Painting, echoing the wildness in which the ship is enveloped.

REALISM

Thread Painting is as versatile as other means of painting and can give a considerable degree of realism to a scene. Envisage an embroidery depicting some fantasy theme, which includes an element of a lifelike nature. Perhaps it could be a picture for a child's playroom. A cartoon character such as Mickey Mouse, dressed up in a magician's cloak and hat, as he was in Walt Disney's film *Fantasia*, could be made of appliquéd pieces of material. The mystical signs on his clothing and other details could be sewn in embroidery thread. In that film he takes the role of sorcerer's apprentice and causes mischief with the magician's spells. You could show him taking an illicit peep into a crystal ball. The realistic scene within is ideal to portray in Thread Painting, in contrast to the unreality of cartoon fantasy.

BLENDING AND SOFTENING

In an earlier part of this book, it was suggested that Thread Painting lends itself to the integration of colours to obtain a soft, gradual transition from one shade to another. It would seem that this is another quality useful to the embroiderer. Hand stitching is usually crisp in nature. Soft effects may be achieved by using fluffy yarns or by painstaking filling of an area in graduated shades of long and short stitch, but neither of these resembles the blending characteristics of Thread Painting.

Clearly, its uses must be many, from totally abstract works to illustrative pictures. It might be useful in depicting the aura of light as it radiates out and diffuses into darkness from a candle flame, or the merging of rainbow colours. Because this blending technique is also by nature a soft effect, one might employ it in an appliquéd work, where a shape needed to be crisp and clearly defined at one side, but blurred and hazy at the other. You could over-sew the soft edge with a machine and, using graduated coloured threads, break down the harsh outline. A good illustration would be a comet, with a clearly defined edge at its head and a soft streaming tail.

UNUSUAL APPLICATIONS

Pictures are most frequently thought of as framed works of art for hanging on a wall. Often they are regarded with reverence and admiration for their artistic merit. Also, in a domestic setting, they can be appreciated because they add to the decorative style of a room and can be said to reflect the personal taste of their makers and owners.

If we think more deeply about the function of art in society throughout history, it becomes clear there are many other roles for it to play. This is particularly true of the present, in keeping with our fascination with novel ideas.

Artists and craftsmen are even now maintaining their tradition of ecclesiastical work, and in bringing modern design and materials together, might well adapt Thread Painting for inclusion in devotional pieces. The themes echoed in religious art are always a creative stimulus. Differing patterns of worship demand a variety of approaches, including story-telling in pictures, meaningful signs and symbols, and a high degree of decoration.

Today's society has, in fact, widened the range of artefacts enormously, taking them beyond the limited ownership of churches, the learned or the wealthy, and enabling all of us to own and enjoy beautiful things. Many of us also find pleasure in making them, and in the giving and receiving of them. There are still few people who can partake of the rarefied atmosphere of fine art, but nevertheless, we make and buy well-designed and collectable objects with unrivalled freedom. These objects might be so mundane in their purpose or so familiar that they are overlooked. Superbly illustrated books or greetings cards come into all our homes. People collect boxes, paperweights, postcards, and so on. Just think what opportunities there are to employ Thread Painting in new ways.

Hand-made greetings cards are always so much more meaningful to the recipient than a bought one, chosen in a hurry. They represent care and effort you are prepared to devote to making a special message and reflect your love or esteem for that person. When was a hand-made card ever thrown away? Cards need not necessarily demand the hours of planning and work that you might put into a full painting. A simple design, with a minimum of stitching, would suffice. You could try a recognisable theme, such as a Christmas tree. The background might be left just painted and special features picked out in stitch.

Any hand-made article takes time to make and requires patience coupled with originality. It follows

'Balloon Seller': fairgrounds provide lively images. The cluster of vibrantly coloured balloons seemed to express the very essence of the fair, with its wheels and carousels floating and radiating outwards in a brightly painted disorder

'Derelict Barn': a drawing using several shades of grey. The sewing-machine makes stitches which can be used in a similar way to lead pencil, or pen and ink

that it will be highly regarded for those attributes as well as its artistic merits. Therefore, it could be especially suitable as a presentation piece, commemoration of momentous events, or a tailor-made gift.

If you have a purpose in mind before embarking on a Thread Painting, this may serve as another factor influencing your choice of design. Book covers including this kind of work can be effective. You could consider a design for a home-made binding to a photograph album. Special photograph collections featuring family weddings, barmitzvahs, graduations and holidays are all splendid subjects to interpret. Your family might like you to make several to accumulate into a matching set for all special events.

Your Thread Painting could be incorporated into a work-box lid, as a gift for someone who loves sewing or knitting. It might be a writing case or make-up box. The theme of your design could echo the personal taste of the recipient to make it meaningful.

In a combined project with someone who enjoys woodwork, you could make some interesting articles which may be considered treasured heirlooms in your family. Imagine, as an example, a jewel case made in wood, with perhaps marquetry or carving. It could be just a tiny box made by wood-turning, with a little lid formed like a round picture frame. You could set a Thread Painting in it as the focal point to the decoration. If you prefer your work to be set behind glass for protection, you could make a piece to be laid in a tray, or bedside table, with a glass top.

These examples are, of course, only suggestions. They are offered not so much to copy, but to stimulate your own ideas for the style and uses of Thread Painting. The range of possibilities is as wide as each individual's capacity as an artist and creative force.

In the same way as a child will take a new colouring set and produce with it his very best work, or a sculptor will make figures that dance from a cumbersome lump of clay, you too can take Thread Painting to its limits, exploring the medium to the fullest advantage.

10

THREAD PAINTING FOR CHILDREN

Opinions vary about the age at which young people can be taught to use an electric sewing-machine. The only sensible answer to this question is that the individual child, the available facilities, and the attitudes and aims of the teacher or parent must all be taken into account. My experience has been that children as young as nine years of age have found the technique within their capabilities.

A class of nine to eleven year olds listened and watched attentively while I talked about and demonstrated my work. Several small groups from that class have since tried Thread Painting for themselves. Some of their work is illustrated on pp90–1. These children all displayed a far greater concentration span than I would have expected, while engaged in a fairly technical learning process. Several worked for three-hour sessions without significant breaks and still came back for more. All were quite capable of learning the safe and effective use of the sewing-machine.

It is generally agreed that new, stimulating ideas for developing children's skills and awareness are welcome in education. The dual concepts of painting and textiles involved in Thread Painting can be seen as an opportunity to further the trend to link aspects of school learning, rather than demarcation of subjects by timetable. Thread Painting crosses the boundaries of specialist subjects and could prove useful in teaching small groups of less academically able children, or advanced pupils who are undertaking examination courses.

Art is essentially a channel of communication, like music and the written and spoken word. Children use their art freely and effectively to illustrate their lives and imaginations. The directness of their pictures can be charming. We should take every opportunity to preserve and develop this uninhibited freshness. To extend the range of media available to young people is to increase their chances of finding one in which they can succeed. It may be that simple Thread Painting methods would be exciting but controllable for some children. It could also be said that this spontaneous effect of machine stitching enhances the directness in children's art.

If you are thinking of introducing young people to this medium, it is worthwhile reading the following suggestions for teaching procedure before formulating your own approach.

It will help in the effective introduction of Thread Painting if you, the instructor, are well organised. The safety aspects alone need to be defined clearly and emphatically. Also, arrangements and facilities in your workroom help to give a strucure to your lesson. Whether teaching the subject to children or adults, the physical arrangements and teaching plan will be challenged by the individual creativity of your students and by their various speeds and unusual ways of working. Always prepare for the unexpected.

(pages 90–1)

A group of children's Thread Paintings: 'Balloons' by Joanna Church, aged nine years, 'Rabbit' by Melanie Beck, aged eleven years, and 'Grandad's Marsh' by Jason Brister, aged eleven years

ARRANGEMENT OF FACILITIES

Try to have separate areas for the different functions. Have books, photographs and sketching equipment well away from paint-pots. Do keep the paint area separate from the sewing-machines and hair-dryers, since water and electricity are dangerous neighbours. Even if your group of children is very small and controllable, these principles apply.

Keep a small box of first-aid equipment handy, just in case anyone does accidentally catch a finger on the machine needle.

Have all electric flex and plugs safely arranged so that no one trips or is in danger from the electricity supply, and do not overload a socket with too many appliances.

Arrange the threads in a pleasing colour order rather than a random mix, so that users may discern the subtle variations between shades and therefore make informed judgements in choosing the best colour for their purpose. Ensure that the used spools are replaced in the same order. For young children, consider their working height at machines and foot pedals. Carry spare machine needles and light bulbs.

SUGGESTED PROCEDURE

It is desirable, especially with young children, to have at least enough adults present to enable careful overseeing of machine practice to ensure that they adopt safe working habits straight away and do not deviate from them. It is also extremely helpful for the prompt sorting out of machine problems so that no child is kept waiting for long. Delays in the flow of their work are likely to lead to frustration and disenchantment. These adults can be parent volunteers who are capable with sewing-machines and who can leave the class teacher free to proceed with the lesson plan. They will inevitably encourage and boost confidence as they go along. Children will respond positively to this interaction with adults and any conversation about their artwork is advantageous.

Introduction to Thread Painting allows teachers to bring in other aspects of art and design along the lines already discussed in this book. A short guide to colour mixing, for example, could be most useful. The links between subjects could also be exploited here. Children are often engaged upon study projects in other school subjects, which would provide excellent material for a picture, and this can be of help when introducing a new technique. It is one less hurdle to jump if the inspiration for a design is already established and your pupils have plenty of sources of visual information to work on.

You should demonstrate briefly the sequence of events in Thread Painting and have an example or two to show. Involve the children in your demonstration as far as possible. Depending on the age and receptiveness of your students, you could discuss the qualities of Thread Painting and start them thinking creatively.

Take your students quickly to the stage where they can make a start on the painting. When the first student is ready for instruction about the use of the sewing-machine, you could draw the whole group around. With younger children, earlier discussion on this topic might be forgotten. Demonstrate the use of each model, emphasising the safety aspects. As each child takes up a place at a sewing-machine for the first few sessions, have an adult check that the safety routine has been observed and understood. Machines are powerful and can do damage to children's fingers. Your teaching plan here begins to depend upon the creativity of each child and upon your hopes and aims for the session.

A first piece of work may take a child between three and seven hours of intensive work. Provided he or she has a relatively trouble-free work pattern, with adult help in technical matters, there should be no problem in concentration. In my experience, the hardest part was persuading children to stop at the end of a session.

The illustrated examples are either first or second attempts by children who were largely unfamiliar with a sewing-machine. Their response was most encouraging. They have all become adept in a short time at the use of the machine for this purpose. They have all understood to varying degrees the similarity with the crayoning action. Most impressive of all was their response to the selection of coloured threads which must have seemed like a vast colouring set containing several hundred shades. In the rabbit picture, the artist has carefully chosen as many tones of pebble colour as she could find and put them together successfully. The child who made the balloon picture has used colours of great intensity. She also showed a particular fascination with my range of threads, spending some time scrutinising their order of arrangement and discussing them. The picture of the trees represents the distinctive lushness of greens in nature. It portrays a field surrounded by a high hedge, with overhanging trees, and owes much to the child's own knowledge of this place.

I have also included my daughter's picture of her teddy bear, which was her first attempt at Thread Painting. She has used an electric sewing-machine before in a conventional way, but the free needle embroidery technique was new to her. She is eighteen years old and is studying art at college.

While this piece of work represents the opposite end of the scale of young people's work, it is indicative that the technique is usable throughout the age groups.

There is already considerable interest in the technique among home economics and art teachers. It is likely that young people with their agile fingers, receptive minds and developing imaginative powers can produce exciting new images with the Thread Painter's palette.

'Hill Village in Andalucia': Thread Painting has much in common with the pointillist technique of applying pure colour in small dabs onto the canvas, to preserve richness and intensity. I have used a similar dotting method with complementary coloured threads. The Mediterranean clarity of light and characteristic landscape lent themselves as subject matter in this attempt to emulate the painting style of Georges Seurat, one of the great French Post-Impressionists

11
SOME QUESTIONS ANSWERED

The most frequent comment from beginners in any new technique is that 'it is easy when you know how' and the mastery of Thread Painting is no exception. If you, the reader, are going to give the suggestions offered in this book a try, you will be without further guidance or encouragement unless you join with a group of people with the same aims. Clearly, while teaching yourself a new subject using a book as your only source of information, there will come moments when you will benefit from extra help.

During the course of my own work and in teaching my technique to others, certain problems and questions arise. In this short section, I have set out some of the most frequently occurring points and have endeavoured to offer likely solutions. I cannot cover every eventuality and new students are good at finding problems hitherto unencountered. It is to be hoped that the following will prove useful in keeping your work flowing with the minimum of frustration. Above all, do not be alarmed at the catalogue of potential problems which I have listed. You would be unlucky to come across many.

DRAWING STAGE

Alteration required in pencil mark on fabric

Light pencil marks can be gently erased from most smooth surfaced fabrics or painted over successfully later. However, carbon paper marks, transfer pencil, felt pen or heavy lead pencil can show through. For this reason, only light drawing is suggested and minimum work is required at this stage. If your drawn design is very wrong, you can either turn your fabric over or discard it and start again. Calico (my favourite fabric) is inexpensive enough to throw away without too many regrets.

Traced picture comes out in reverse

It is an easy point to miss when tracing your design. Nothing can be done about it after the event, but it may not matter as long as your picture does not include any lettering, numbers, and so on, or feature a subject which is meant to be recognised. Some designs will work equally well in reverse.

PAINTING STAGE

Colours run together by mistake

The cause is clearly that you failed to dry one colour before applying the next. With thick paint, such as acrylics, you can sometimes go over the blemish to hide it. It may also be possible to cover the error under stitching.

Colours become dull when dry

Painting on to fabric is rather different from using a paper ground. Often the cloth is absorbent and has a slightly fluffy surface. Rich paint colours can soak in and when they are dry, appear less vibrant than you had intended. This is most likely to happen with any initial layer of paint. Quite often, if you go over it again, the pigment will stay richer and not soak in so much. Do not forget that the threads you are going to stitch on have a distinct richness and lustre which will bring a dull painted background to life.

Paint will not spread in a consistent flow from your brush

Brushwork on paper is relatively easy. A loaded brush will spread the paint readily. Fabric tends to have a more resistant surface and brush loads seem to dry up quicker. You will need to use a good quality paint brush with plenty of spring in its hairs. A stiff or floppy one will be of little use. Also, make your paint reasonably fluid and keep your brush fully loaded with paint. If you still have problems, dampen that particular area of fabric with clear water first.

Painted errors need correction

Thick paints will probably cover mistakes or it may be possible to hide them with threads. Major mishaps may necessitate discarding your work and starting again.

Paint rubs off on the threads when stitching

Some paint types may not be entirely suitable for Thread Painting because of their powdery nature. You should experiment, if in doubt, before using them on a valued work of art. School powder paints may fall into this category.

THREADS

Are there any types of thread suitable for Thread Painting other than polyester dressmaking thread?

You are, of course, at liberty to try out any kind of thread. The following points should be noted.

Cotton or silk may be susceptible to fading in daylight, and can deteriorate in storage or in your work. Yarns are made in various thicknesses and you may have to change your machine thread tension setting for each yarn. Manufacturers use various methods of twisting the thread and of mixing man-made and natural fibres, making a product which will perform differently in use from other types of yarn.

Certain slubby or fluffy threads may only be couched down and not passed through the machine needle. If you wish to use a special thread, such as a metallic twist, it is best applied by winding it on the shuttle bobbin and stitching your picture the wrong way up. This is complicated as you need to draw out the pattern in reverse and in register with the rest of your picture, on the back of your fabric, as a guide to sewing.

Can I use two coloured threads at once?

Yes, if you can pass two fine threads through the eye of a machine needle, you can apply a dual-coloured effect on to your work.

MACHINE STITCHING

Needle snaps while sewing

If your needle becomes bent or is misaligned with the hole in the needle plate it will break and probably make a snag in the metal parts of the mechanism below. Needles can easily be replaced. Check regularly that your needle is straight and sharp. Try not to pull at your work too eagerly while the machine is operating. This may cause the needle to bend so far out of true that it catches on a machine part, rather than passing safely through the needle plate. Just occasionally you may find that a sewing foot attachment works loose in its housing and the needle collides with it.

Threads knot at the back of your work

This is usually due to a lack of tension in your top thread. Check that you have lowered the presser bar to engage the top tension. Make sure that your top tension setting is correct. If it is too loose, it will allow a free flow of threads to the needle and cause knots below.

Thread wears and breaks during sewing

Any small snags and burrs of metal within the hook race, or on the needle plate, might be wearing at your thread. These burrs can be polished smooth by your service engineer, or sometimes rubbed down with a fine emery cloth at home. Another cause may be a misaligned needle which passes too close to the mechanism, thus chafing your thread. Occasionally, the thread may have a slub or knot in it which will not pass through the needle. The only remedy for this is to use a good quality thread whose manufacturer guarantees no knots or slubs or any variations in the thread diameter.

'A Day Last Summer'

'Summer Lane'

Stitch not forming properly	Check for correct top and bottom thread tension. You may need to tighten the fabric in your hoop. Any slackness will cause the work to whip up and down with the passage of the needle and prevent the good stitch forming at each cycle. Use of a darning foot helps to promote a regular stitch formation. Check that the bobbin, its case and the hook are correctly positioned and that there is not too great a build-up of lint in the mechanism.
The under-thread appears on the picture surface	Your bobbin tension needs increasing in balance with the top tension (see p19). Alternatively, the bobbin thread may have become disengaged from the tension mechanism and needs rethreading.
Stitches pile up in one place causing a knot	Without the feed teeth to assist the passage of fabric under the needle, it is up to you to keep the work moving. If you let it remain static, the needle will continue to apply stitches in a mass at one point on your work. Check that there is nothing obstructing that freedom of movement, such as a loop of thread caught up on the machine, or that the hoop is too large to move any further in one direction under the arch of the machine.
The needle housing or presser foot collides with the hoop	You are probably trying to work too close to the edge of your fabric and the machine will not comfortably pass so near to the embroidery hoop. Turn your work around for easier access to those tricky corners. When planning future pieces, either make a slightly smaller picture or use a larger diameter hoop. You could find that constant rattling of machine parts against the hoop will do damage and it is best avoided.
Mistakes in stitching need correcting	Quite often the easiest way to remedy poor stitching is simply to go over it. You need only unpick if the error is going to show. That is fairly rare. When unpicking stitches, avoid cutting the foundation weave of the background cloth.
Can I use any built-in stitches or special attachments?	Your model of sewing-machine may have facilities which you could adapt for Thread Painting. It is really up to you to explore the full potential of your own materials and equipment and to use them creatively. The technique of Thread Painting is relatively new. There is plenty of scope for further ideas.
The needle comes unthreaded as the machine starts	You should leave both the top and bottom thread ends at least 8cm (3in) long when cutting off and it is best to hold these ends away from you as the machine makes the first few stitches. Then you can trim the ends close to the fabric.
Do I need to cut joining threads frequently?	It is necessary to stop your work occasionally to trim the extraneous threads. This only needs to be done when they begin to obscure your vision and prevent you from evaluating the work.
Major machine faults	Seek the advice of the professional if you have any doubts about the effective running of your machine.

STRETCHING YOUR WORK

Your picture has not returned to its flat state even after stretching

Provided that you have used a paint which will not run, you can dampen thc buckled area after it is stretched. Place it under a weight to hold it out flat and wait for it to dry. Failing this, you may need to stretch it again, using heavier board and stronger thread.

MOUNT CUTTING AND FRAMING

Your knife tears the surface of your mount board

A blunt or jagged blade will not cut well and may damage the mount surface. Renew the blade whenever it becomes dull.

Your results do not appear squared and true

Check all your measurements, including the outer corners, ensuring that they measure 90°. Make sure your equipment is accurate. You are unlikely to be able to rectify a poor mount, but will know how to improve the next one.

PROJECTS

In previous sections of this book some of the possible starting points for Thread Painting have been explained. If you are new to the medium, it is as well to allow some practice time in which to develop your picture-making and technical skills. However, your initial enthusiasm, which is the most precious ingredient in any creative process, should not be permitted to decline through a tedious period of dull exercises. As soon as you have mastered the handling of paint and machine to a degree of reasonable familiarity, you could try a simple picture.

The following section offers a series of ideas for Thread Paintings. The explanatory notes for each picture project indicate its suitability for beginners or for the more accomplished. You might wish to start with the first project and work your way through them, or to pick one from the range which you feel suits your taste and ability.

The projects have been developed for you to interpret as faithfully as you wish. They may be followed closely throughout. It is necessary to bear in mind that, unlike transfers for hand embroidery or painting by numbers, the individual marks, stitch types and positions and colours have in the first place been produced as the picture went along. They are naturally somewhat unplanned. Therefore, it is impossible to guide you with any rigid directions. You will need to look at the illustrations and use them as examples in conjunction with the advice in the text. There are no hard and fast rules about Thread Painting, except those which you formulate for your own ease of working.

These projects have also been devised to offer more freedom to those readers who do not wish to copy examples down to the last detail. Each can be used as a suggested theme to interpret in your own

'Poppies in Wheat'

103

way. The first picture is of a familiar English landscape with very few elements to identify it, or to make it too complex for a first attempt. Using the same theme, you could alter it slightly by changing the position of the clump of trees or the slope of the land. You could add a distant church steeple and suggestions of a hidden village. The field of corn could be at an unripe stage where the poppies are dotted among green stems. The flowers might be daisies or buttercups in the meadow. If you have access to pictures, or are able to find real countryside offering another view on the same lines, so much the better. It would be possible to follow my directions for the given picture by taking them loosely and adapting the general advice to suit your design.

When you have selected your project, you will need to prepare adequately, even if interpreting the theme differently. You should read the text through to familiarise yourself with the sequence of working and any special points which might arise. The next step is to collect together all your ongoing requirements for Thread Painting, as detailed in Chapter 1, so that your paints, sewing-machine and small items are always to hand. Add specially chosen threads, fabric, hoop size and equipment, which are specified at the beginning of each project.

Consider the end product and its purpose so that you are ready to work to the most suitable shape and scale. It may be possible to trace directly from the diagrams, but you are most likely to be obliged to use one of the suggested methods of translating the design on to the fabric (see p65).

Even if you are following the projects closely, do not forget that your rendering is as much a work of art as the original. Any mistakes, barring mishaps, can easily be covered up, put right or, even better, regarded as examples of your own artistic interpretation. It would be impossible to copy any of these pictures exactly. There is certainly some value in trying to emulate any artist's work, since you will learn far more about his skills and qualities than simply looking and admiring.

Whether you decide to follow these projects closely or to dip into them, interpreting the ideas in your style, there will hopefully be something in this section to inspire you. It is also to be hoped that this book will encourage you to persevere beyond the beginner stage with confidence, and to become an enthusiastic and accomplished artist in this attractive new medium.

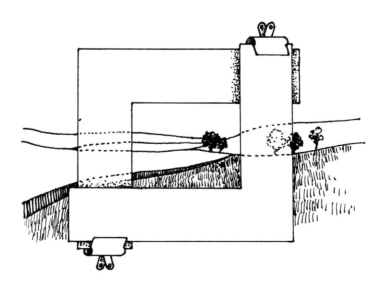

POPPY FIELD

Materials and Equipment

◇ Sewing-machine, ready-wound bobbins, scissors, needles.
◇ Paints or dyes in at least the basic range recommended (see Chapter 1). Brushes, pencils, palette, water-pot, tissues, hair-dryer.
◇ Fabric suitable for background for the project.
◇ Hoop, about 25cm (10in) for the poppies.
◇ Threads: soft, distant blue-greens; richer greens in light and dark shades; corn colours of several shades; two or three bright poppy colours, including pink. You may need about twenty different colours to make this picture.

This picture has been chosen as an easy starter project for you to try if you are attempting Thread Painting for the first time. It is a simple composition featuring a narrow band of detail in the distance and a greater proportion of rolling cornfield coming into the foreground. Random splashes and clusters of red poppies enliven the otherwise static scene. The picture space is divided in strips from side to side, but the upright image shape counteracts this predominant lateral banding effect.

The subject matter is familiar to most of us. Landscape and poppy flowers seem to inspire emotions of great joy and sadness and to evoke a sense of timelessness of our English countryside. They have frequently been depicted in art and offer a splendid subject for the newcomer to this technique.

You should begin by selecting some fabric and an embroidery hoop. To start with, it is wise to choose a hoop of 25cm (10in) diameter or less, although this type of picture will look well on a larger scale, too. Stretch your fabric on the hoop.

Draw a rectangle (on the right side, ie with taut fabric flat on the table) to mark out the extremities of your picture, leaving at least 1.25cm (½in) space inside the rim of the hoop. Use a series of light pencil marks to divide up the picture area, referring to the diagram for guidance. Note tentatively with your pencil any details you may wish to include.

Begin painting in the colour as soon as possible, following as closely as you wish the directions given here. Start with the sky. Mix white with a tiny speck of blue to make a pale sky-blue. Paint this over the whole sky area. While this is still wet, mix a slightly darker blue. Starting from the top, paint over the paler shade, gradually merging and blending the two shades until the sky appears bluer towards the top. If you look at the sky outside on a clear day, you will notice that it is very light near the horizon and much darker high above you.

Dry the painted sky (with a hair-dryer for speed). Now proceed to paint in the narrow strips of distant trees and fields, drying each patch before you put on another colour. These little areas need to be clearly defined and if you allow painted sections to run into each other they will blur the effect. The row of trees furthest away ought to be pale blue-green in colour to give the appearance of distance. This is another phenomenon you may notice in reality. The trees of the middle distance are nearer and better defined. They will need to be painted with richer greens, including some light and dark shades to indicate their fulness. As you move forward through the scene, you will be able to paint in more noticeable blobs and brush strokes, giving detail, form and interest to your picture, and providing a lively texture upon which to base your stitches.

Once the distance is painted and dried, you can give the whole field a wash of pale corn colour, this time keeping the field wet and blending in variations of the original colour. You can allow the colours to run and blur in this instance because it will give the effect of soft rustling corn and gently rolling landscape.

Fig 30 Diagram of 'Poppy Field' showing the main divisions of the picture area

A touch of pink fading into the cornfield gold, near the trees, will be enough to suggest a blush of poppies too far away to distinguish each bloom. The foreground needs to be more weighty and detailed. Use brush strokes in an up and down movement to introduce richer colours nearer to the bottom of the picture.

Finally, using a finer brush loaded with various shades of pinks and reds, add blobs for patches of poppies. These should only be suggestions of flowers, not evenly spaced. They should be more distinct and larger in the foreground.

Select coloured threads to complement the painted work. You will need at least two shades for the distant trees, and up to five shades for the nearer ones. These should range from light to dark and could include some blue-greens. The cornfield will also benefit from the use of several different shades to make the large field space more interesting to look at. Choose more than one poppy colour.

Start by stitching the distant trees. Select a very narrow zig-zag. Turn the picture sideways to give a vertical texture. Do all that is possible in the first colour. Add other pale blue-greens to that area.

Change colour for the furthest field. Alter the stitch width to zero (running stitch). Keep the image sideways to you. Fill in the field with backward and forward straight stitches so that they will lie across the field when the picture is viewed the right way up. Fill in each of the distant fields the same way, using colours which are sufficiently different to show up as separate areas.

Using a narrow zig-zag in a random way, by turning and twisting the image under the needle as you sew, fill in the nearer trees and bushes with as many shades and tones of green as necessary to show light and shade. Allow the trees to slightly overlap the sky and distance to make them appear closer.

The cornfield is worked with the image sideways. Pushing to and fro under the needle as you sew, start with a very narrow zig-zag near the trees. Work your way down to the front of the picture, allowing the zig-zag to increase in width until it is at its widest near the bottom. Extend the zig-zag width even further by rocking the work from side to side while stitching. This will make a straw-like effect in the foreground. Blend coloured threads together to build up shadow and contour in the field.

Lastly, apply tiny dots in a small zig-zag with poppy colours. As the flowers are to appear larger nearer to the spectator, make the zig-zag wider towards the bottom of the picture. Stitch one or two poppies clearly and with some accuracy to provide detail.

The illustration was worked on a 25cm (10in) hoop. The image measures 14 × 19cm (5½ × 7½in), and when mounted with a card border it will fit into a 25 × 30cm (10 × 12in) frame size.

BLUEBELLS

Materials and Equipment

◇ Sewing-machine.
◇ Painting equipment.
◇ Background fabric.
◇ Hoop, 23cm (9in) is suggested.
◇ Threads: a group of about ten different greens, light and dark shades, plus lime-greens and blue-greens; four or five earth colours for branches and bare soil; a group of blues for flowers.

This effective picture gives the impression of complexity by virtue of its entangled textures. In fact, the design is non-committal and would be most suitable for a beginner. The drawing skills required are minimal, since none of the component parts are clearly defined. Wobbles, missed stitches and errors can be stitched over and will appear intentional. The picture space simply has to be organised into general areas of shade and colour, with the introduction of a few more specific details such as a partially seen tree trunk, some twisted branches and a suggestion of some clearly defined leaf shapes.

You should begin by dividing your picture shape into patches of light and dark by pencilling roughly as shown in the diagram. Mark the position of any main features such as tree trunks. Remember at this stage to consider the need to make a pleasing arrangement on your given space. You can follow the diagram as loosely as you wish. When you are sketching, try to think out the work with your pencil. If you want marks for grass, then allow your pencil to give a grassy effect. If you are drawing twigs and leaves, follow the line of growth or make blobs and patches as appropriate. Keep in your mind the stitching process, and while drawing or painting you will already be forming some notion of how you are going to use the machine to enhance the image.

Following on from your sketching, block in with

paints the colours and tones. Using your brush as a texturing and drawing implement, try to develop contrasts in colours, light and dark values, as well as various types of leaf, bark, soil and blossom. Aim to make the distinct areas of your picture different from one another so that the viewer can imagine picking his way across the clumps of bluebells and under the trees.

You can show your skills in handling paint here. There are places for you to apply colour to damp areas, allowing the shades to blend together for a soft effect. Also, you will need to paint some patches crisply to create sharp edges and clear detail.

The apparent complexity of this image makes it difficult to decide where to start stitching. The usual advice applies. Begin in the most distant regions of your picture. In this case, it should be behind the trees. Stitch general areas of light and dark greens in an all-over texture, allowing your approach to be quite random. All you are doing here is filling in an approximate background on which to stitch tree trunks, branches and leaves. Establish the variations in colour and tone within this back-cloth.

Now start to work forward as if the components of the picture were real. If the tree trunks come next, they should be stitched on top of the background, using a wide zig-zag closely set.

Superimpose overhanging branches, twigs and leaves in the right order, as they are situated in nearness to the onlooker. Decide how the leaves grow and hang, as well as their shape. For instance, the horse chestnut leaves fan out in a sort of hand shape and grow horizontally, whereas willow leaves are long and thin and usually hang delicately down. Of course, it is not necessary to define every leaf, but you should select your stitch width and direction to echo the characteristics of the subject matter in your picture.

Sew in parts of bare earth which show, remembering any likely texture, stones or leaf mould, and showing any shadows under the trees and close to plants. Keep your daylight coming from one source direction, making all shadows fall at the same angle.

Now stitch in the tufts of bluebells and undergrowth, working your way forwards through the picture space. Follow the growth habit of each type of plant, choosing a corresponding texture for stalks, strap-like bluebell leaves and spires of tiny dots for the flower spikes. Vary the colours so that you give the impression of highlights and shadow among them. As you come forward, make your stitches more deliberate, your texture larger and the detail better defined. Perhaps as a finishing touch, you could sew one or two bluebells as precisely as you can, in the foreground, so as to identify them clearly. Use carefully controlled stitches here, in the same manner as the final exercises in diagram 7 on p21.

Fig 31 Sketch for 'Bluebells'

The woodland theme is one of considerable scope. You could paint a much larger version with a wider view through a wood. The changing seasons give plenty of possibilities. Winter trees are beautiful and autumn brings wonderful colours. You could depict a springtime image including primroses, or a little close-up of a hedgerow with violets, buttercups or daisies.

When you choose your theme, you should collect together plenty of pictorial help in the form of photographs or sketches so that you can create your picture with convincing detail and not just rely on memory.

You will need a good supply of coloured threads encompassing the whole range of shades and tones for your version of this picture. 'Bluebells' will probably take up to twenty different colours, including several greens, some very dark tones of green-browns, three or four blues, and beige and creams. Do not forget to include a few really bright light shades, which you may only use in small quantities, but which will lift the picture and give it that extra sparkle.

My example was worked on a 23cm (9in) hoop. to an image size 11 × 16cm (4½ × 6½in) and will fit a standard frame size 20 × 25cm (8 × 10in).

DORSET RIVER

Materials and Equipment

◇ Sewing-machine.
◇ Painting equipment.
◇ Fabric background.
◇ Hoop, 30cm (12in).
◇ Threads: a large group of greens, bearing in mind that this picture has an accent on light and shade; some warm browns and some greyish browns. You will need at least twenty shades. Don't forget to include one or two vibrant colours such as lime-green, emerald and duck-egg blue.

Here is a project which is slightly more ambitious than the previous two (see overleaf). It combines much of the random effect described in the text for 'Bluebells' with a representation of reflections in water. In order to make a recognisable attempt at portraying water, you should have plenty of photographic reference material. It would also be helpful to prepare yourself by looking at the way other artists have expressed water in their paintings. Library books may be helpful here.

A good deal of dark rich colouring has been used to create the reflections on the surface of the stream as it flows peacefully under the canopy of trees and out into the sunlight. The river is used in the composition as the main element, attracting the attention of the observer and inviting him to take an imaginary journey beyond the scene.

The overall composition begins with the horizon line across the picture, but it hardly features in the final work. You should lightly sketch it in and then establish the lines of the river banks. Next mark the position of the main tree trunks and their attendant masses of leaves. Begin to form some impression of important patches of deep shade and specific textures.

Most of your preparatory work will be in the painting stage since there is very little detailed drawing involved.

Begin by painting in the light blue patches of sky and add touches of the same colour to the part of the river which is in daylight. As with previous projects, your brushwork should echo texture and direction. Special attention should be paid to the fluttering leaves, smooth tree bark and linear grasses, and particularly to the way you paint and stitch the water. It is helpful to remember that water surfaces are horizontal except when disturbed. Totally calm or gently rippling water is often best expressed by straight brush or stitch marks.

As you paint, move forward through the picture, putting leaves in front of sky, tree trunks on top of background, and so on, until you can add the closest fronds of greenery and grasses.

Notice how in the picture, and with certainty in any photograph of your own from which you may be working, the areas of colour reflected in the water correspond to the positions of features in other parts of the image. They are mirrored, but appear a little blurred and distorted. Our perception of the surface of water is further confused by what we can see through it as well as these reflections, just as we can see passing traffic in a shop window while being able to discern the display of goods within.

You should begin to stitch from distance to foreground as normal, concentrating on grouping your textures and colours to give a semblance of sunshine and shadow. Superimpose some of the trees with twigs and branches. Work the river surface before you put in any overhanging branches. Last of all, put in the plants on the nearest bank so that some overlap the water to create the impression of foreground detail.

My picture featured lush summer greens since these scenes of dappled sunlight appeal to me. If you wish to follow this design closely, you should collect a good tonal range of several types of green. You might, for example, select some lime-greens, olive-greens and another group based on those with a bluish bias. You will also need some soft browns for the trees, earth and reflections.

I use greens in many of my pictures because they form a natural background to the type of subject I like to paint. If you choose to adapt this project, or to make up your own design on this theme, you might prefer to use autumn tints or to depict your trees full of blossom.

'Dorset River' was worked on a 30cm (12in) hoop and will be suitable for mounting and framing in a 30cm (12in) surround.

Fig 32 Diagram of 'Dorset River'

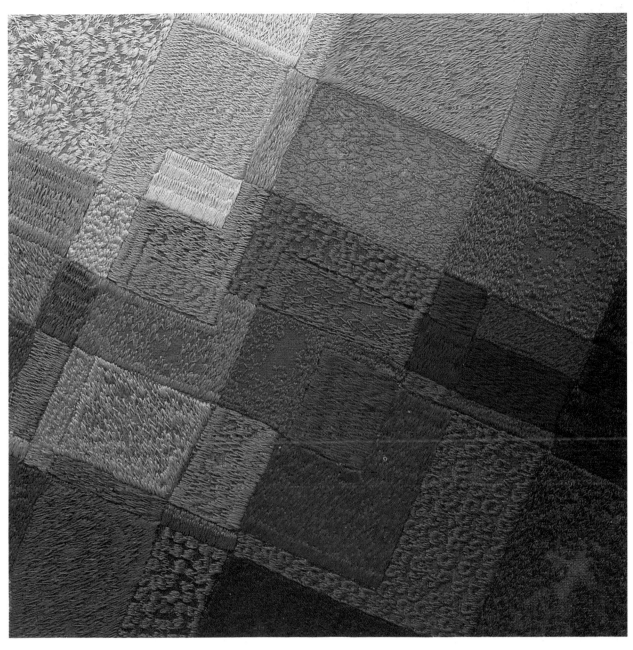

'Hot Spot'

'Dorset River'

HOT SPOT

Materials and Equipment
◇ Sewing-machine.
◇ Paints.
◇ Background fabric.
◇ Hoop: size suitable for your picture.
◇ Card for template, cutting knife, ruler.
◇ Threads: the illustration is based on reds
and requires a very large range of pinks,
reds and reddish browns, but your choice
will be influenced by your own design.

Abstract pictures give the impression that they were plucked out of thin air with no apparent pre-planning. They often depict a simple concept and therefore look easy to produce. Despite that appearance, such a painting requires as much care in its design as for a representational work, including the development of an initial idea, composing the elements into a pleasing arrangement and choosing a suitable colour scheme. It is often true to say that the simpler the image, the more it shows up the imperfections.

This project is purposely open-ended. The instructions are of a general nature, enabling the reader to create his or her very own design, which will, of course, be unique. It is based on the purely abstract concept of geometric shapes and colour 'families' (see p115).

Work directly on to your stretched background fabric and draw an outline denoting the limits of your picture. It can be any practical shape: square, circle, oval, diamond, etc.

Make a cardboard template of any geometric. shape, which might even echo your outline. Lay the template across the picture area randomly and move it about until its edge cuts the space in a pleasing way – no matter if it only takes a small bite out of the corner or a bold slice through the middle.

Keep moving the template and draw round it until you have a series of divisions which are, in your opinion, satisfactory. Bear in mind the principles of composition which might be helpful. For instance, it is usually true that regular sizes and shapes are repetitive and boring. Try to give your design variety, including larger areas where the eye can rest. Step back and look at your whole picture while planning it to get an idea of the overall effect, and adjust it where necessary.

While you draw, start thinking about a colour scheme and how you could make it work in your composition.

My example is simple. It has a square outline and the pattern is formed with a right angle which repeats itself at irregular intervals. There is a uniform slant of about 65°. It was drawn without careful measurement and therefore has some in-accuracies which soften an otherwise rigid pattern.

The colour scheme was chosen for its powerful impact and also because I so seldom get a chance to use so many delicious reds in one picture. After all, even an abstract work must surely have a message, and this is a celebration of colour.

You could have great fun putting together a group of colours which excite you. If you do not know how to begin, take a look at the arrangement of threads in their point of sale displays in haberdashery shops. See how a row of related shades look well together, but if you isolate one, it loses some of the quality which pleases the eye. It is the skilful grouping of colours which attracts. Each shade enhances the group. The larger the collection, the more visually interesting it becomes.

Make your final selection of threads before you begin to paint. You may have several ends of spools which will form the basis of a good colour scheme. Add new shades, including some subtle ones to act as a foil for the richer ones. You could work in light and dark tones, or keep to an even tonal range.

The hints on colour mixing in Chapter 4 will prove useful, particularly when you wish to achieve special variations. The painting process needs to be carried out with similar attention to the overall effect as the drawing stage. Your choice of neighbouring colours is important. Rather than just painting arbitrarily, consider what the result will look like.

Since the directions given here are essentially just a guide, it is not desirable to tell you specifically what to aim for, but to leave it to your own individuality. The picture illustrated here might, for example, have been made in an approximate chequerboard pattern of light and dark shades, or have featured complementary colours. It could have started at one side in blues and wandered across the picture space, turning to pinks as it went. The permutations are endless. The only guarantee is that you are sure to enjoy thinking it out.

The stitching of this kind of picture is influenced by considerations of texture, stitch direction and choice of colour. At its simplest, you could just stitch using a shade to match the paint, in a single zig-zag width, at different angles throughout. The light falling on the angled threads would give enough sheen to make the work interesting. However, there is a wealth of texture to employ and it is up to you to exploit your machine's capabilities to the full.

You can begin sewing at any point and proceed in any order, depending on the effects you want. There is no visual representation of reality, so you are only governed by whatever is practical for your own ease of working.

Simply follow your instincts and invent stitched textures to suit your needs. You could even set up your machine with feed-dog in operation to use the satin stitch facility, basting stitch, tailor tacking foot, inbuilt patterns, or other special devices that are available to you. You might add effects which can only be produced by hand embroidery.

Your abstract pictures may be turned to good use. These richly decorated surfaces make wonderful insets into box-lids, album covers, and so on. You could incorporate someone's initials into the design and make it into a very special gift; or adapt a theme, such as a company logo, marriage date, ecclesiastical symbol or anniversary colour, as for a ruby wedding.

Hopefully, this project will give you much pleasure and encourage you in the development of your style and individuality.

The illustration here is only a sample for you to see. It is based on a size suitable for a 30cm (12in) square frame and was worked on this scale for ease of production. You are, of course, free to choose any size and shape which is practical for your purpose.

SUNSET

Materials and Equipment
◇ Sewing-machine.
◇ Paints.
◇ Plastic sprayer.
◇ Fabric background.
◇ Hoop, 25cm (10in).
◇ Threads: collect a range of subtle colours in the grey-brown area, making sure that you have some with a yellow bias, some which look reddish, some green; include very light and dark shades, but not pure black.

Generations of artists have found inspiration in dramatic skies which illuminate the landscape in some remarkable way. The sight of a sunset can evoke all sorts of emotions in us. It marks the passage of time, causing us to stop and marvel at its beauty and reflect on our own experiences.

You might like to try out the theme for yourself. My picture is a simple one, avoiding complicated cloud formations and concentrating upon the smooth graduation of sky colour and an unusual angle of light from the sun. You will need to spend plenty of time in careful painting and perhaps proportionally less in the stitching stage. This kind of image is most suitable for anyone who is adept at handling paint and who prefers the more obvious use of paint in conjunction with thread. The stitching stage can be quite simple. The sunset theme could also be easily adapted to your own design.

The subject matter works well on any scale because of its powerful impact. You could be brave and try a large picture, or it would be equally successful in the form of a miniature. A large picture will probably necessitate moving your hoop from place to place across the image while you work, if it is too large to fit into the biggest available embroidery hoop.

Sketch out your basic design on to the fabric background. Try not to use too much pencil in the sky area because the grey dust from the lead will probably mingle with the paint and spoil the clarity of colour.

Begin painting the sky and work it until you are entirely satisfied with the result since this is the most important feature of the picture. The illustration shows a smooth blending of colour from the sun outwards and upwards. It requires careful paint mixing on a palette so that there are no streaks of unblended pigment in the work. Where you are using a thick paint medium, such as acrylic, it is advisable to mix with a palette knife before applying the paint with a brush. To obtain the smooth transition from shade to shade always keep the painted surface wet while working. If you allow one edge to dry before adding its neighbouring shade, you will produce an unwanted jump from colour to colour.

A little plastic hand-spray filled with clear water is useful for damping the picture surface. They are available from cosmetics counters of most chemists and cost only a few pence. They are refillable, being manufactured for spraying hair lacquer and toilet water. Another alternative would be a houseplant mist sprayer from a garden centre.

In the sunset picture illustrated here, the only crisp detail in the sky is the sun itself, which was painted last with a fine brush, making a neat distinguishable shape against the surrounding colour. The sun is the brightest element and has a high percentage of white paint in it to give it the necessary luminosity.

Next, you should paint in the detail which is most distant. This will form the horizon and link with the sky. In the illustration the distance has a bluish-purple haze which represents the moisture in the atmosphere and is almost as pale as the sky itself. As you work forward through the picture space, the colours should become deeper and richer.

The other aspect to note when painting a picture showing an unusual light source, is the colour change caused. In the illustration, the normal day-light colours of fields and trees, as they might have been at midday, are made darker and less colourful by the weak rays emitted by the sinking sun. You can imagine that a few minutes later there would be no sunlight, and therefore only very dark shapes in blues and blacks, with little distinction between them. Again, you should mix the paints carefully before using them, being sure to get a suitable shade each time.

The stitching stage of this work is much less complex. You do not need to add any threads to the sky, preserving its painted smoothness. Use it to contrast the tree textures and solidity of earth. Select some subtle greys and earth colours for your threads. Stitch in the distant detail with a tiny texture. Your zig-zag can be set at a fraction wider than straight stitch. The distant fields should appear quite smooth. A straight (running) stitch in a horizontal direction will achieve this.

Do not forget to work from distance towards the foreground. As you come nearer, increase your texture. The closest field of cut stubble can be achieved with an ever-widening zig-zag following the rough lines caused by harvesting. You will need to turn your work round 90° to make the zig-zag formation appear vertical in your picture.

Even in a painting as dark and subtle as this one, you should consider using more than one shade of thread to mingle together on the surface. The human eye is less able to distinguish between dark colours, probably because of the reduced light reflection for the eye to receive. It is all too easy to classify this group of colours as black. Your picture will benefit enormously if you avoid using absolute black and substitute some wonderful velvety rich, dark threads. If you look at them and use them in good strong daylight you will soon see the difference.

Using these subdued colours and an encrusted texture, add foreground detail such as brambles, grasses, twigs and leaves. Let your choice of stitch width and direction copy the characteristics of the particular plants.

In the picture, the trees in the middle distance and foreground break into the sky, giving emphasis to the textural and tonal contrasts. They play a major part in the overall dramatic effect, but are comparatively easy to stitch since they are almost in silhouette. You should try to give specific qualities to these shapes, working from drawings or photographs. Observe the angle of branches, the particular tree trunk framework and the pattern of the leaves. Try not to repeat the same shape in another tree. Aim to give a convincing authenticity to your picture. Refer back to the original source to refresh your memory of the overall mood and to maintain some of the important detail which you might otherwise have omitted. Of course, copying faithfully from your notes is too rigid an approach, so do leave yourself plenty of scope to improve your picture artistically while trying to preserve the essence of your inspiration.

Since this theme is likely to produce dramatic images, you should give special consideration to the choice of mounts and frame so that the visual impact is not lost or overpowered. Make the choice from as wide a selection of mount colours and frame types as possible, aiming to complement the colour bias of the work. Again, avoid using plain black because it will look lifeless against the luxurious dark threads.

The illustration was worked on a 25cm (10in) hoop for a 30cm (12in) square frame.

Fig 33 Sketch for 'Sunset' with dotted lines indicating the direction of stripes of cut corn

GARDEN

Materials and Equipment
◇ Sewing-machine.
◇ Paints.
◇ Fabric.
◇ Hoop, 25cm (10in).
◇ Threads: you will need about thirty different colours. Collect several greens for the leaves, with dark, medium and light versions of each type of green; plus a series of pinks, reds and purples. Select these flower colours to go well together in your picture.

The theme of the old-fashioned garden lends itself in many ways to the Thread Painting technique. Gardens are full of textural variations. We gather together a profusion of plants with a multitude of different leaf shapes and growth patterns, and we fill our gardens with a great tapestry based on background foliage and flower colour. All this rich and random texture is governed by the rigid framework of the ground plan and attendant architecture. There are distinct styles of garden design, each offering the artist a different approach. The formal knot garden of Tudor times features a strict geometric layout, with small flower beds each delineated by a low clipped hedge. Later fashion often entailed great avenues and vistas, with lakes, temples and grottoes. Cottage flower borders give the impression of a riot of shape and colour, without a rigid planting plan. Japanese gardens, which pay special attention to the contrasts between natural and man-made elements, are also splendid subjects for Thread Painting since they have already been planned with many of these aesthetic considerations in mind.

I have chosen to illustrate part of a herbaceous border for this project. The principles involved are similar to those in the 'Bluebell' picture in that the overall effect is all important. There is no specific drawing ability required. You just need to map out the principal areas and shapes. There are simple ways of altering the picture to suit your taste and ability. You might, for example, add a suggestion of a cottage partly visible in the background by fitting it in the plain area top left of the picture. You could alter the colour scheme, making the flowers predominantly blue, yellow, or whatever you choose. You might feature a gravel or flagstone path winding through the plants, or a trellis or pergola for climbing roses.

Despite the apparent intricacy of this image, it is quite a simple basis for a beginner and could even be successful worked from memory. It is a suitable subject for a small painting and can be highly decorative. I have chosen to make a circular picture, but the theme would look good in any shape. You might prefer to work on only a small part of my design to make a miniature.

Start by sketching in the main areas which divide up the picture space. Establish the shadows. As you draw, allow your pencil to respond to the qualities in groups of plants so that you begin thinking out the tapestry effect right away. There is no need to draw each leaf or flower shape, provided you know roughly what you plan for each area.

Paint in the next stage with dabs and blobs as a way of preserving the textural feeling. It is as well not to be too precise in paint. The idea is not to produce a faithful rendering of the scene at this point, but to develop scope and inspiration for lively stitching using the paint as a guide. Your aim should be to use the paints to establish the most pleasing arrangement of colours and tones.

You have an opportunity here to use some rich and startling colours. Remember to employ a hairdryer to speed up the process if you want to keep colours crisp, or to paint over still wet patches if you wish to blend them.

As the garden theme can involve a rather jumbled general image, it is all the more important to work from the distance to the foreground, both in paint and stitch, emphasising the impression of one clump of plants in front of another. Variations in colour, texture and shading are vital devices to use as contrast, and if they are used skilfully in the design will help define elements of the picture and portray space.

Before you begin to stitch, you should ensure that you have enough coloured threads. You will need as many different greens as possible, remembering that for most trees, bushes and clumps of plants you will need light, medium and dark shades, and that the kinds of green vary from plant to plant. It is helpful to vary the shades within one flower type, too. Flowers also tend to catch the sunlight and shadow. They can fade with age or they may even grow in a mixture of colours from one seed packet. Some coloured threads need only be used sparingly and so part-used spools will be sufficient for anything but the larger patches. The picture illustrated contains over thirty different colours.

I started stitching the illustrated work in dark shadow under the bushes to form a background, using a narrow zig-zag in a random manner. No attempt was made to cover up all the green paint. The bushes were completed with several other greens and a cream with pale pink in tiny blobs to make an impression of blossom. This touch of pink helped soften the stark shape and formed a visual link with the predominantly rosy colours in the rest of the picture.

The pale greens in area A were worked next, using a wide zig-zag and with the picture turned around 90°. This formed the grassy texture behind the pink and blue dots, which were then laid on top.

Area B, featuring red and pink flower spikes, was then worked, any visible background colour being added before stitching on top. The exact order in which you should stitch your picture will be your own decision because of inevitable variations from my example.

Moving forward through the picture, the white flowers in area C were stitched, the dark green being put in first. Then came the large fan-shaped leaves near the front. These were achieved with small zig-zags radiating outwards from their centres, with light green near the tips.

Both the leaflets and daisy-type petals in area D were made by widening and narrowing the zig-zag as the picture progressed (see exercises on p21).

The finishing touches were the flower centres. Addition of these little details always seems to complete a picture, and I use them like punctuation marks to identify specific parts of my work.

The overall effect of such a full image could be thought fussy, but I have endeavoured to avoid this by including a space empty of stitches as a rest for the eye. I have given consideration to variation of scale, colour grouping and tone.

This theme can involve a good deal of thread changing and fiddly work, but it is a splendid excuse to use all those glorious colours and patterns. These pictures are usually highly decorative and make attractive gifts, greetings cards, book covers and box-lid inlays. The possibilities are endless.

'Garden' was a small picture made for a round or square frame of about 20–25cm (8–10in).

Fig 34 Guide to 'Garden' showing different textural areas

WINTER TREE

Materials and Equipment
◇ Sewing-machine.
◇ Paints.
◇ Background fabric.
◇ Hoop, 30cm (12in).
◇ Threads: pale pearly greys, subtle yellow-browns; two or three dark browns for the bare trees; some rust shades for the nearest field.

Here is a project which makes a feature of the sewing-machine's capacity as a drawing tool, in combination with the texturing facility already evident in the previous pictures.

The subject matter is an obvious candidate for drawing and could even be done in monochrome, like a pen and wash picture or sepia-toned photograph. Winter landscapes offer a wonderful range of subtle colours in contrast with the stark contours and the distinctive patterns of leafless trees. The season also brings mists, clear crisp sunlight and dramatic skies.

You may develop the theme illustrated here into your own composition. As always, it is advisable to make careful observations beforehand, giving yourself plenty of visual information to select from. The illustrated example of a winter landscape is a favourite theme of mine. The tree is impressive for its almost perfect outline, which is unusual in my neighbourhood where most trees bow to the prevailing winds. I have used the misty grey woods as a foil upon which to set the growth pattern of the tree, allowing its topmost branches to be more clearly silhouetted against the sky. The soft blue-greys contrast well with the tree.

While these main features are shown as a band across the space, the nearest field is therefore made to curve broadly round to relieve the monotony. It has been further accentuated by the dark strip of ditch bordering the field and by suggestions of a ridged contour to the ground. The curve leads the eye assertively into the image. The main tree is placed just off centre. It is dominant in the space and would look too mechanical in the middle. An oval outline was chosen to echo the tree profile. You can see that quite simple examples of both linear and atmospheric perspective are used as key devices in the plan.

This picture has a slightly abstract quality which was suggested by the actual view. I have perhaps exaggerated this aspect and missed out some extraneous detail. It would be very easy to make a yet more abstract version. A further interpretation could be made by introducing appliqué work. An overlaid arrangement of nets and tulles might give a gentle smoky effect for the background woods. Bands of textured fabric interstitched with Thread Painting could form hedgerows, and the front field could be made from a more heavily textured cloth and even quilted down to create those ridged contours. You could Thread Paint to draw the tree and bushes, and to enhance the foreground.

To work the project for yourself, pencil in the basic divisions on to the fabric. Mark in only the most prominent branches and tree trunk and draw a lightly dotted line around its outline. It would be wasted effort at this stage to put in more of the fine branches. If you are drawing your own choice of tree, remember to make it convincing by careful observation of the way it grows, and the angles and characteristic patterns that it makes against the sky.

Begin as usual by painting the sky, then pay some attention to the subtle greys in the distant woods, giving them a little light and shade, and soften the colours towards the sky. Paint in the distant fields, using colours which are not too rich, but distinguishable from each other. Make sure that they are dry before continuing.

With a dark colour, perhaps brown and blue mixed, but definitely not black straight from the tube, paint the main branches of the tree and bushes. Do not attempt to fill in all the branches and twigs yet, but with a fine brush, make some inward-facing dashes around the outline to identify the tree shape.

As you add colour to the foreground field, remember to think out a suggestion of texture with your brush. In such a potentially stark picture, you will most likely need to develop some detail in the field surface nearest to the onlooker, to give it extra interest.

For similar reasons you will need to have to hand sufficient thread shades to bring surface interest to an otherwise plain image. The greys especially should be selected for their variety. Try to avoid dead greys derived from absolute black. Look instead for those with a hint of colour, as well as light and dark ones. It does not matter if they seem similar at a distance. They will blend together softly and produce just that hazy effect you require.

As always, begin stitching in the distance first. In this case, you should start with the grey bank of trees. Choose a small zig-zag, and twist and turn your work as you go along so that the stitches do not lie all in one direction. Blend in the grey threads, leaving as much paint showing as you wish. For an extra touch of detail, put in some slightly more distinct tree trunk and branch shapes using the same greys on top of the first stitching.

Working forwards, stitch in the fields and hedge in sequence, until you get to the ditch boundary. A running stitch across the picture or a tiny zig-zag will be useful for filling in the distance, always remembering that your texture can become bolder as it gets nearer.

For the tree, choose a dark brown of sufficient richness to stand out against the background. Stitch the main branches strongly in a satin stitch, gradually narrowing the stitch width as the branches near their ends. You can add secondary branches as you go along. When the principal structure is complete, change the thread to a slightly lighter one, set your zig-zag to about 2mm (1/8in) wide, and lay in a network of twigs by random stitching almost all over the tree canopy area. Form the characteristic outline and establish areas of dense growth. Finally, with your original dark brown, over-stitch some more branches to build up the final effect. The bushes can be made in the same way.

Lastly, you should develop the front field and ditch with a variety of textures, which can include wide zig-zags laid on in vertical direction. You should emphasise the shadows which delineate the ditch and field furrows. The close-up texture towards the bottom of the image can be picked out in special detail and may include touches of colour almost as dark as the tree in order to echo that weight and detail to balance the design.

Earth-coloured mounts in contrasting tones, coupled with a gold frame, suit this picture well. You are not limited to an oval outline, but can use a rectangular secondary mount to fit a standard mitred frame.

This picture was worked on a 30cm (12in) hoop and will be displayed in a double mount. The inner card will have an oval aperture to fit the image and the outer will be rectangular and darker in tone. The frame size will be 35 × 40cm (14 × 16in). However, you can make the picture any size or shape, provided you consider the design in relation to it.

Fig 35 Simplified sketch for 'Winter Tree' (not to scale)

CORAL REEF

Materials and Equipment

◇ Sewing-machine.
◇ Paints or dyes.
◇ Plastic sprayer and an old tooth-brush.
◇ Hoop: note that if you do a very large
   picture the hoop will need to be moved
   about as you work on the image.
◇ Fabric background: you might find a ready-
   dyed piece to suit.
◇ Stranded cottons and crewel needles for
   hand working the fish.
◇ Threads: range of blues, greys, greens and
   purples, with some sharp colours, and
   others in dusky subtle shades for stitching
   the coral formations.

The mysterious and exotic undersea world offers a vast topic to explore in painting. One only has to open a book describing oceanography, or look at a film about deep-sea diving, to realise its potential as a picture-making and design theme. The wonderful colours, sleek glistening fish, grotesque fantastic shapes of marine creatures and coral formations are stunning examples of the range and perfection of life on earth. Our attempts to reproduce that beauty in art are likely to be weak in comparison. Nevertheless, the subject is so inspiring it is worth a try.

'Coral Reef' is a combination of paint, Thread Painting and hand embroidery. Large areas of the calico have been left in the painted state, as a smooth contrast to the encrusted coral formations, which are done in Thread Painting. The shadows of fish are just painted in. The silvery fish are worked in hand embroidery stitches, with stranded cottons. I wanted to give these fish as shiny an appearance as possible, as distinct from the rough corals. The whole picture is larger than my usual scale since I felt that the subject warranted plenty of space.

To achieve the extra size, the background fabric was stretched taut on to a piece of card and stapled into position in order to keep it flat while painting the design. To suit your purpose, you could make a smaller picture and use the right size embroidery hoop. The example illustrated here was so big that it was necessary to keep moving the hoop to another part of the design while stitching.

With only a very light sketchy drawing, mark in the main area of coral and the fish outlines. Move on to the painted stage as soon as you can. Wet the background fabric with clean water. Overpaint the sea with a soft brush, loaded with fluid blue paint. Dry this before continuing. Mix up some blue, green and purple paints, inks or dyes, into a liquid state. This is applied using a small plastic spray bottle to spread the colour evenly. You could use an artist's air-brush, fixative diffuser, or even dab it on with a sponge. The aim is to blend smoothly the sea colours over the canvas, to obtain gradation in colour and intensity, without any harsh streaks or patches. You may need to dampen and dry the surface alternately as you go along, to keep the effect soft.

About half way through this process, paint in the silhouettes of the distant fish, using a dark colour. Continue to spray or dab the sea-water colours on top of the fish, making them merge in tones with their background.

Next comes your chance to excel with colour mixing. My picture shows a group of coral formations in the blue–green–purple range. I used Ultramarine, Dioxazine Purple and Monestral Blue, with some Viridian, Burnt Sienna and white. The shades achieved by mixing these in subtle variations seem to be harmonious and to suit the theme. I worked in acrylics, mixing them on a palette and dabbing them on to the picture with a tiny palette knife. They were then blended and softened with a sable brush.

When you are satisfied with your arrangement of corals, you can paint the silvery fish, going to very little detail, but establishing their shape and tone.

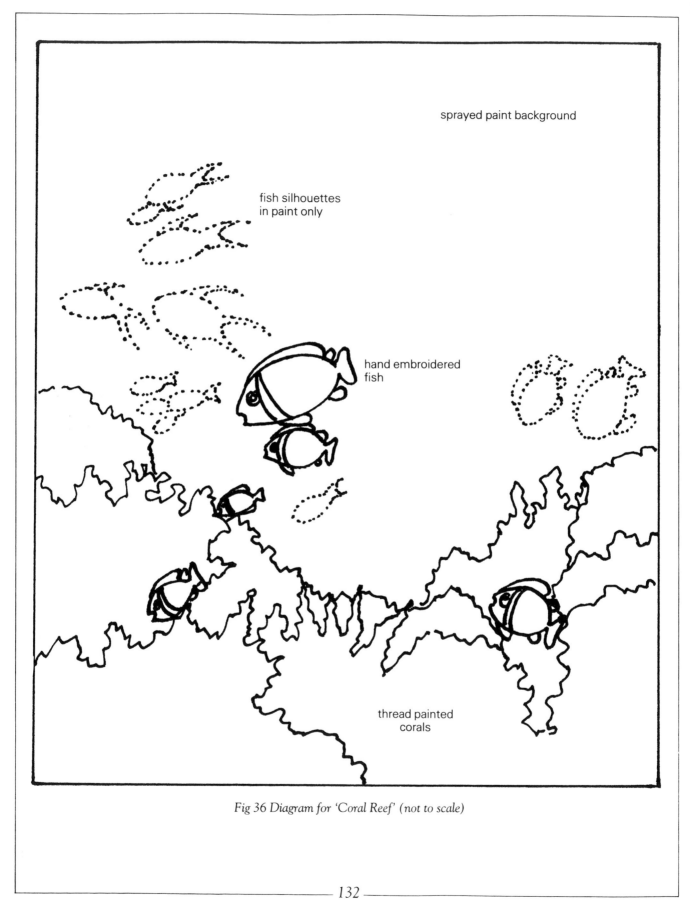

sprayed paint background

fish silhouettes
in paint only

hand embroidered
fish

thread painted
corals

Fig 36 Diagram for 'Coral Reef' (not to scale)

Dry this stage. Lastly, take a stiff paint-brush or old tooth-brush, load it with white or light blue paint, and flick it with a thumb so that it spatters the surface. This takes a bit of practice. You could make a trial run on a piece of scrap paper. You should achieve a scattering of bubble-like blobs to enhance the watery quality.

When the work is dry, take out the staples, if this is how you stretched your fabric for painting, and fit it on the hoop, ready to sew. If your picture is large, you will have to keep moving the hoop in order to work all parts of the picture.

Choose the coloured threads from the more subtle shades available and in keeping with your painting. You will need different tones and one or two threads of greater richness and clarity than the rest to bring sharpness to your image. You will also need a group of stranded cottons and crewel needles for hand stitching the fish. They should be in keeping with the colour range, but sufficiently different to distinguish the fish from their surroundings. Again, select some shades for light and shadow.

Begin by stitching the coral growths with the sewing-machine. Select a width of zig-zag which will give a texture in the right scale for your picture. Start at the points furthest away from the viewer, in just the same way as a landscape. The distant corals may be less easy to discern and can therefore be worked as shadowy shapes.

As you come forward in the picture space, you should add overlapping layers of stitching representing different types of corals. Remember to give them shape and shadow. Texture them differently, too, by using various widths of zig-zag, and by twisting and turning your work as you stitch. You may like to refresh your memory by looking again at your reference material, picking out further information

about marine encrustations, and giving the picture that added touch of realism.

You may wish, however, to develop your theme into more of a design, paying less attention to the realistic aspects. The subject matter invites an abstract approach, being full of pattern and colour ideas, which could be embellished as you go along.

When you have completed the machine texturing, slip the embroidery hoop on to the work in the right position for hand stitching the fish. You may prefer to have your hoop the other way up at this stage. The choice of hand embroidery must be suitable for the task. For example, a shiny surface would be best created by tightly packed satin stitch or long and short stitch, the stitches being laid in the most effective direction to catch the light. Your fish may have spots, stripes, prominent scale or gently blended markings. Look at fish patterns and then at samples or diagrams of embroidery stitches to evaluate the kind of marks you could make with each and to match them with the fish. Stitches can be adapted. Try an open fly stitch in rows, touching at each extremity, and see how it can be used for a scaled effect. Keep a clear distinction between the roughness of Thread Painting and the rich exotic appearance of the fish.

Finally, you might like to go back to the sewing-machine and add one or two branches of coral overlapping some of the fish to show them swimming among the corals, like the one illustrated, in the bottom left corner.

Your undersea picture, with its glowing depth of colours, would look well in an unusual mount and frame. You could possibly extend the coral painting on to the mount. It would be worth a visit to a professional framer to seek his advice and to find out what types of materials are available.

ROCKERY

Materials and Equipment
◇ Sewing-machine.
◇ Paints.
◇ Fabric, for background.
◇ Fabric, to simulate rock for appliqué.
◇ Pieces of card, sponge, sprayer, for further patterning of rock appliqué.
◇ Hoop: size to fit picture.
◇ Threads: various greens and browns; flower colours to match your design for alpine plants. Light and dark shades are important.

There is a randomness to natural rock formations which the enthusiastic gardener often attempts to reproduce in alpine gardens. These rocks form the architecture around and among which the plants are set. Alpine plants sometimes grow in neat clumps or ramble over the contours of their neighbouring stone blocks. Some have leaves which grow in beautiful patterns; others put forth masses of attractive flowers which show off in contrast with their glaucous blue foliage and the stony environment.

You can use these contrasting characteristics, matching them with embroidery techniques, and making a particular feature of your newly learned Thread Painting skills. Books on garden plants will show you the many types of alpines and give you some initial ideas for development into a picture.

My example was based on a foundation of appliquéd fabric for the rocks, set against a dark painted background and interspersed with alpine plants worked in Thread Painting. The rocks were cut from a scrap of material which was already a subtle shade of greenish grey, but which was enhanced with sprayed, dabbed and brushed patches of light and dark paint. Pieces of this fabric were stitched to the picture and the gaps between were painted dark earth shades to set the plants against. The rocks were further textured with Thread Painting and the plants added towards the end of the process.

Your picture need not follow my example exactly since you may have your own ideas to develop, but the basic planning and sequence may be similar.

You will need to select some cloth which you feel to be a suitable colour and texture for chunks of rock. They could even be bits of bouclé material, or slubby furnishing fabric, glazed cotton, sail-cloth or an abstract print. Do choose a fabric which will not fray badly when cut, but will remain workable as small appliqué pieces. A very heavy denim was chosen for this example, which fortunately cut into crisp workable shapes.

Keeping this fabric entire to begin with, you should give it a rocky appearance in paint or dyes. Rather than make a wild guess about rock patterns, take a look at pictures of geological formations, or better still, the real thing, even if only in a garden centre. Remind yourself of the sort of marks, cracks and facets on various kinds of stone.

Mix up some paint in a group of colours and tones in keeping with your chosen fabric. You could spray colour on, possibly using a torn sheet of paper as a masking device. Shift the paper around and spray randomly each time. This should produce a mottled effect plus crisp edges to the areas of paint. Paint can also be dabbed on with a sponge, brush or finger. You might print with the edge of a piece of card. Cover the fabric with rock-like patterning and let it dry.

Next, you should pick parts of this painted fabric which are most effective and cut out several chunks for rock shapes, and arrange them on the picture space. They might sit next to each other or even overlap. The main thing is to achieve a pleasing arrangement, leaving some cracks in between. With the rocks loosely pinned to the background, paint darker shades between them by dabbing the brush to make a rich crumbly soil texture. Stitch down the edges of the rocks, except where you may wish to have a rock overlapping the plants, to give the impression that it is in the front.

Look carefully at the patterns you have made on the surfaces of the stones and pick out in Thread Painting any cracks, patterns and fissures which you feel will give them greater realism. You might also like to embellish them with touches of lichen or moss, using the sewing-machine. Complete as much of the rock and soil structure as possible so that you have the foundation of the alpine garden as it would have been before any plants were set into it.

At this stage, you may wish to return to painting and apply dabs of colour to the areas which will be occupied by plants. This is a further planning process to clarify the colour and types of plant as a basis for stitching. Look at reference pictures of alpines. Select them for their shape, leaf type, colour and flowers. Be sure that they are suitable to fit in your picture. Consider whether they sit well in between the rocks, if they climb or trail decoratively over the shapes you have created, and whether they make a good pattern within the picture space. The stony background with its angles and smooth facets should provide a splendid contrast against which to place the delicate blooms. This picture has only limited perspective, so you are fairly free to begin stitching where you wish. It is still important to remember that any part of your work which is intended to appear behind another should be done first. Overlap the nearer object, be it plant or stone.

You might also consider that there is shadow between leaves and under plants, where they cut out the light. Use several tones of leaf and flower colour to achieve this light and shade effect.

Choose the stitch width and direction according to the kind of texture each plant exhibits. Many alpines have small woolly or spiky leaves. Some are soft and downy or have attractive leaf whorls. Try to match your stitching to the feel of each plant and to follow its growth pattern. Also try to respond to the shape of rock and allow your plants to belong in their environment, following the crevices and falling across rock faces, filling the available space as they would in life.

This theme encompasses a wide range of techniques along with Thread Painting. Hand embroidery stitches could be added to embellish the work. Centres of flowers may be improved with french knots or bullion stitch. It might be fun to include a special feature like a snail, ladybird or bee in hand stitch using stranded cottons. This attention to detail could put just the right finishing touch to your picture.

'Rockery' was worked to fit a 30 × 35cm (12 × 14in) frame when mounted appropriately.

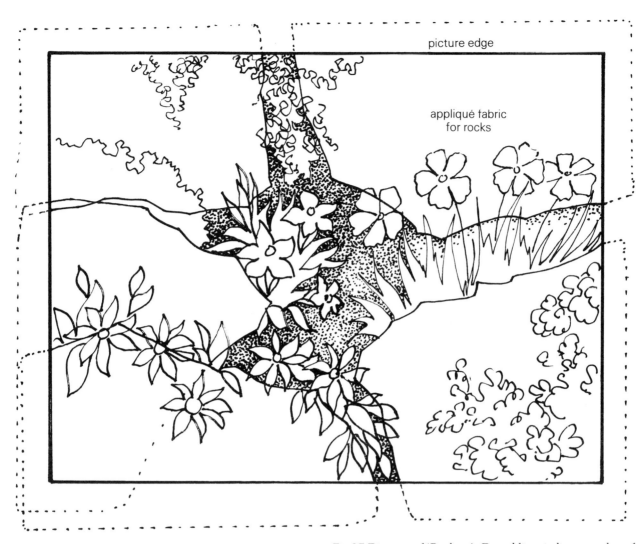

picture edge

appliqué fabric
for rocks

Fig 37 Diagram of 'Rockery'. Dotted lines indicate patches of
appliquéd fabric

TEDDY BEAR PHOTOGRAPH ALBUM

Materials and Equipment
◇ Sewing-machine.
◇ Paints.
◇ Background fabric.
◇ Hoop.
◇ Threads: look at the teddy bear you are working from and select fur shades to match, including highlights and shadows. Collect colours for paws, eyes, nose, ears, jacket, bow tie, etc, and any background colour.
  To make the book cover:
◇ Adhesive (non-latex).
◇ Card, knife, scissors, ruler, pencil, set square and protractor.
◇ Fabric for the cover (strong weave, non-stretch).
◇ Ready-made photograph album, to cover.

This teddy bear album is a project with a difference. It combines Thread Painting with the craft of bookbinding. You may choose to carry out the idea as a picture only, or as a cover for a bought or homemade album, depending on how adventurous you feel. The illustrated example has been designed and worked by my eighteen-year-old daughter and is a development of the theme 'Ricky Bear and Friends' (see p59). It is her first Thread Painting, which she carried out without any guidance except for the accumulated knowledge of the technique through observation. We worked together on the making of the book, copying as far as possible a Victorian album for style and construction. Her teddy bear drawings decorate pages throughout the book.

After reading through this commentary, you should decide how you wish to execute this project. Clearly, if you are going to frame the image as a picture, the procedure will be the same as for the other projects. You may like the idea of turning it to use as a cover for a ready-made book and will need to buy a suitable album or scrap-book to decorate. Consider the size of your purchase, making sure that you can easily do a Thread Painting to fit within its overall dimensions. Alternatively, you could make your own book with sheets of paper or thin card for the pages. Library books might be of technical help to you when attempting to put your own album together.

You are, of course, free to plan your design differently to suit any purpose. This teddy bear seems to be a lovely idea for an album containing a photographic record of a child's first years. It breaks from the traditional pale pink or blue new baby theme, using stronger colour and a more dominant, though still nursery-based image. The background is left largely unstitched, except to give texture and weight to the blanket upon which the bear is sitting. His fur and knitted jacket depend heavily upon Thread Painting. The image has been stretched and mounted conventionally. Ordinary mount card has been painted gold for the inner frame and the outer mount has been covered with blue denim, chosen for its matching colour with the bear's jacket.

You should begin by lightly sketching out your picture in pencil, making sure that you have worked out the correct size and shape for your book cover. Draw a real teddy bear if you can to get a good likeness. Colour it in carefully, deciding where you can leave painted areas unstitched. Aim to achieve a sense of furriness in the paint. Pay special attention to changing shades of light and dark in the fur, and to characteristics of eyes, nose and other recognisable features.

In our picture, stitching began in the blanket so that the bear could be superimposed on it. His fur was worked before his knitted coat, which had to

appear as if it was worn over the top. The fur looks particularly effective because attention was paid to the angle at which it lies on the bear's head, limbs and body. His jacket was given a knitted look by using several shades of blue thread in conjunction with a knobbly texture. The buttons are made from bits of felt, painted and stitched on. His leathery paws are created with the machine set for satin stitch and using several shades of brown. The whole work is quite simple in essence, but detail and character have been brought out with a little extra effort in observation and careful working.

MAKING THE COVER FOR A BOUGHT ALBUM
You may have your own ideas about making a book cover, and, with resourcefulness and ingenuity, will be able to carry on this project without further help. These instructions describe the process used to make the teddy album in the illustration, substituting a bought album for our home-made one.

You will need some good card, one piece of which is chosen for its colour and will be used for the inner mount around the image. Ours is painted gold. Your book should be covered in a firm fabric which is not prone to fraying when cut. Choose this also to match the picture.

Use a sharp craft knife and scissors, a suitable adhesive (not latex based as it may deteriorate and mark your fabric), a straight edge, ruler, set square and pencils.

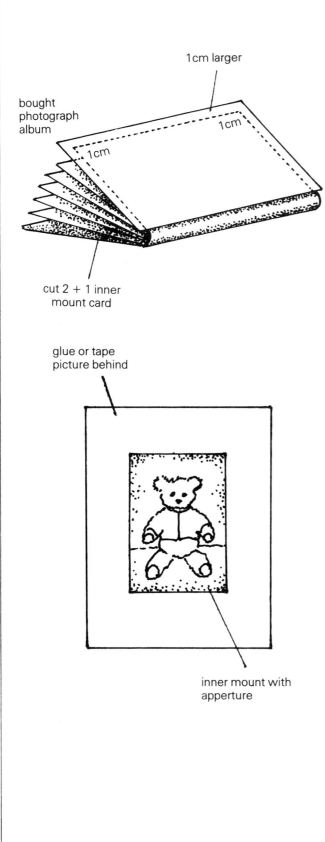

1cm larger

bought
photograph
album

1cm

1cm

cut 2 + 1 inner
mount card

glue or tape
picture behind

inner mount with
apperture

First, stretch the picture in the usual way, then proceed as follows:

1 Your bought photograph album or scrap-book will have its own cover, which should be fairly thin as it will become quite bulky when your work is attached. Measure and cut two pieces of card, plus another of your chosen inner mount colour, each piece being up to 1cm (½in) larger at the top, bottom and one side than the overall dimensions of the book. Be sure to cut the corners at 90°.

2 On your inner mount, measure and cut an aperture to fit the image (see Chapter 8 on mount cutting). Fix your picture into it with sticky tape.

3 On one of your plain pieces of card, measure and cut an aperture larger than the first (how much larger is a matter for your judgement). This will form the basis of the fabric-covered mount.

4 Cut a piece of fabric about 4cm (1½in) larger all round than the outer mount. Lay it face down on the table and place the mount on top.

5 Keeping the work steady, cut a small window in the fabric cover, within the aperture, and snip almost into the corners.

6 Glue along the inner edges of the aperture and neatly fold the fabric flaps over to make a tidy finish from the outside.

7 Pick up the work and centre it over the image plus inner mount. Glue it into position (still with the outer flaps of fabric hanging loose).

8 Replace the double mount with picture in situ, face down again. Snip off the corners of outer fabric flaps at about 45°, but a few millimetres away from the tips of card.

9 Fold the flaps over both pieces of card and stick them down on the inside, making tidy edges. Pay particular attention to neatness at the corners.

10 Cover the last piece of plain card with fabric in a similar way to make a back cover for the book.

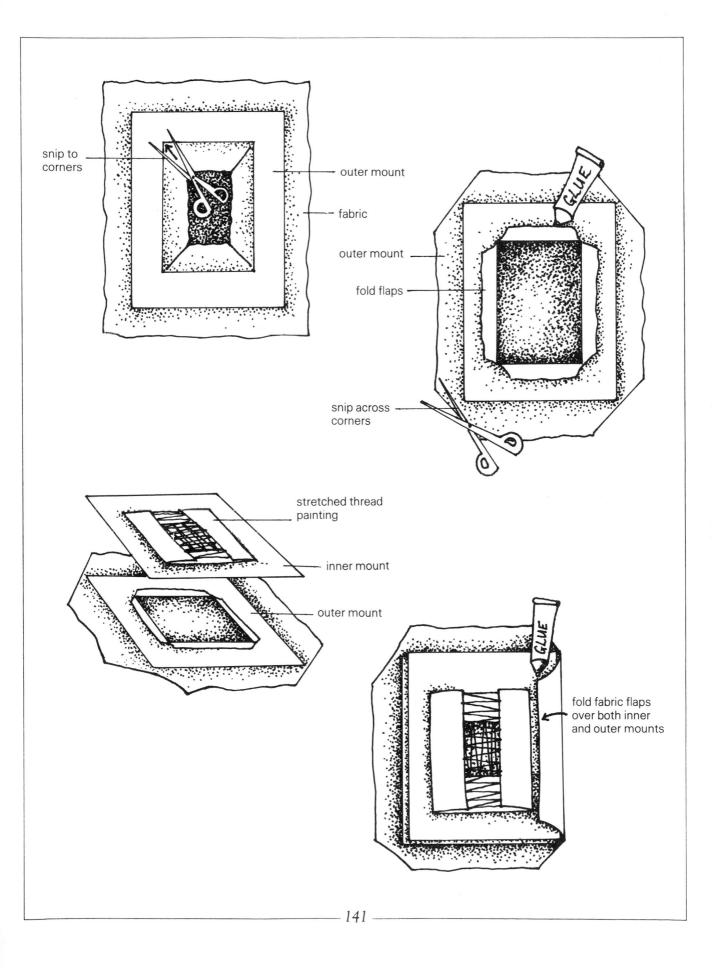

snip to corners

outer mount

fabric

outer mount

fold flaps

snip across corners

GLUE

stretched thread painting

inner mount

outer mount

GLUE

fold fabric flaps over both inner and outer mounts

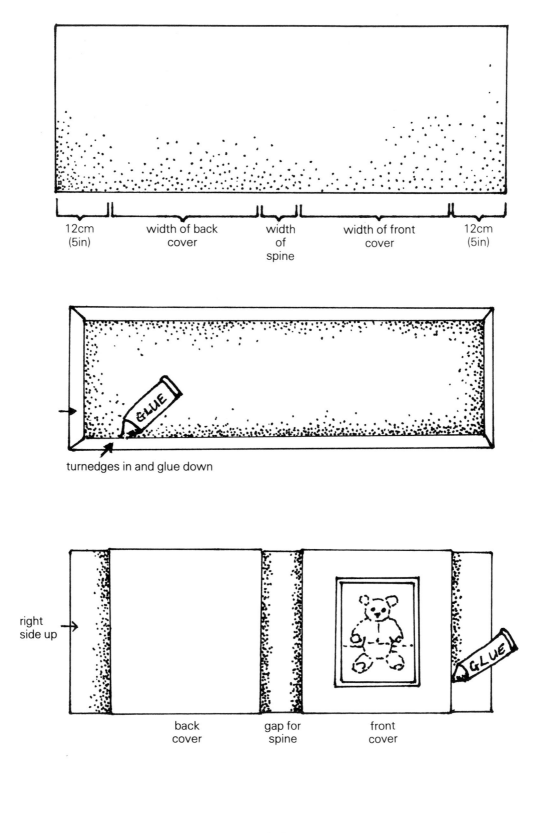

12cm (5in) width of back cover width of spine width of front cover 12cm (5in)

turnedges in and glue down

right side up

back cover gap for spine front cover

11 Measure out a new strip of fabric for joining the back and front together and to form an attachment mechanism to bring cover and album into one unit. This long strip should measure approximately 12cm (5in) + width of front cover + width of album spine + width of back cover + another 12cm (5in). Its width should be a few centimetres more than the height of the book.

12 Turn in the long edges until its width is the same as your album height and glue them down. Turn and glue the ends to about 2cm (1in).

13 Place this fabric strip right side uppermost and centre your front and back covers on it, leaving the correct sized gap for the spine and the end flaps loose. Glue them down securely on to the strip and wait for the whole to dry thoroughly.

14 At this stage you have a choice of methods of attachment to the album itself. You can simply use adhesive to stick the cover over the original, folding in and gluing the fabric flaps. Alternatively, you can neatly stitch the flaps as you turn them in, to join at the top and bottom with the outer cover, making pockets front and back. This should enable you to slip the cover on and off at will, like a book's dust jacket.

album

fold flaps round

GLOSSARY

Air brush	A piece of artist's equipment for applying a fine, even mist of colour to their work. The apparatus consists of a spray mechanism, a reservoir for the liquid colour, and a means of propelling this through the jet at high pressure, either from a compressed-air canister or a motorised pump.
Appliqué	This is a popular embroidery technique for adding pieces of material to a piece of work, by stitching them down, either invisibly or decoratively.
Bouclé	Knitting yarns with a looped thread effect.
Chenille	A yarn which has a characteristic velvet texture.
Complementary colours	Colours which occur opposite each other in the colour wheel are said to be complementary. Combined, they represent all three primary colours. In juxtaposition, they have the visual effect of maximising each other's colour qualities.
Couched threads	Yarns of all types, however unusual, can be added to an embroidery without threading them through a needle or pulling them through the background cloth. They can simply be laid on top in any pattern and stitched into place with a matching or contrasting thread, thus using to the full effect the texture of your yarns.
Feed teeth; feed-dog	The feed teeth are a simple device on your sewing-machine for pulling the fabric through at a regular rate during stitching. Their action is synchronised with the needle cycle. The feed-dog refers to the mechanism as a whole and is located under the needle plate.
Focal point	In the artistic sense, this term refers to an area of a picture which attracts the attention of the onlooker.
Hatching and cross-hatching	A means of filling in an area or to depict light and shade, when limited to the use of a linear drawing tool, such as pen or pencil. Hatching is a series of finely drawn parallel marks; cross-hatching increases the depth of tone by a second layer of lines in the opposite direction.
Lint	Fluffy deposits from the regular use of thread, which wears slightly as it passes through the machine. Lint should be removed at intervals from your machine to prevent poor stitch formation and to keep your machine in peak condition.
Mitre	Picture frames conventionally have a mitred joint at the corners. The ends of

each length of frame are cut at 45° and pinned or glued to form joints at a diagonal angle to the picture.

Mount (matt) Pictures which are displayed with a card, fabric or timber surround between the image and the frame are said to have a mount.

Palette This word most frequently refers to the dish or board upon which an artist mixes his colours. However, it can also be used to mean the total available or chosen range of colours in an artist's repertoire.

Presser foot; presser bar Sewing-machines usually operate with one of a selection of presser-foot attachments which fulfil specific stitch functions. They are raised and lowered by means of the presser-bar lever to the rear of the machine.

Radius The widest dimension of a circle is called its diameter. Half of this, ie from edge to centre, is the radius.

Rebate Framers use the term rebate to indicate the depth and width of the space to the back of a picture frame in which the picture, glass, etc fits.

Tambour frame Another name for an embroidery hoop, used mostly for hand work.

Thread tension Both the top thread and that which is supplied by the bobbin and shuttle on your sewing-machine will be fed through during stitching at a given rate. This is governed by the slackness or tightness of the mechanisms through which the needle and bobbin threads pass, giving the required tension.

Vanishing muslin This fine fabric is specially made as a temporary support for very flimsy cloth while it is being worked. The muslin can be degraded in various ways so that it falls from the work, leaving the finished article unaffected. Some types depend on heat, which weakens the structure of the muslin so that it crumbles on touch. Others rely on moisture to bring about the same result. You should follow the manufacturer's advice about suitability and usage.

BIBLIOGRAPHY

Books of all kinds give me much pleasure. They are indispensable sources of information and often offer the seeds of an idea for a picture theme. This list is only a starting point, selected from the great variety of old and new volumes available through libraries and booksellers. They are among those I have found useful in my work.

Clabburn, Pamela. *The Needleworker's Dictionary* (Macmillan (London) Ltd) 1976. Indispensable reference for anyone interested in the history and technique of needlework.

Collins, Judith and others. *Technique of Modern Artists* (Macdonald & Co) 1983. One of the many excellent art history books in my local library.

Cordcroy, John. *Bookbinding for Beginners* (Studio Vista) 1967. Detailed information for those who wish to develop this idea in conjunction with Thread Painting.

Dalton, Stephen. *The Secret Life of an Oakwood* (Century) 1986. A superb book full of wonderful photographs which are guaranteed to awaken the creative spirit.

Friend, David. *Composition* (Pitman) 1975. Subtitled '*A Painter's Guide to Basic Problems and Solutions*'. A helpful work on the subject of composition in painting.

Kornerup, A. and Wanscher, J. H. *Handbook of Colour* (Methuen). A most useful reference, containing a comprehensive series of colour charts.

Norling, Ernest. *Perspective Drawing* (Walter T. Foster, USA). No 29 in the series 'How to Draw'. An easy-to-follow visual explanation of the whole topic of perspective.

Schinz, Marina. *Visions of Paradise* (Thames & Hudson Inc) 1985. A beautifully photographed exploration of the whole range of garden styles. An inspiration to the Thread Painter.

ACKNOWLEDGEMENTS

I would like to thank Perivale Gütermann Ltd for their support and technical advice in the making of this book, the staff and pupils of Freethorpe County Primary School for their interest and enthusiasm in the project, and Gerry Yardy for his skilful photography throughout.

Especial thanks to my family who enable me to devote so much of my time to the writing and illustrating of this book and whose advice, help and encouragement contributed to all aspects of the work.

Perivale Gütermann Ltd will be pleased to supply a list of stockists of their excellent range of Sew All thread, and give advice or technical aspects of thread and machines.

Perivale Gütermann Ltd
Wadsworth Road
Greenford
Middx UB6 7JS

Gütermann
Colour Collection

Selected for Gütermann by Liz Hubbard

Bracken	Chestnut	Forest	Greenwood
Harebell	Heliotrope	Heron	Iceberg
Marigold	Ocean	Oystershell	Poppies
Rambling Rose	Sunset	Wallflowers	Willow

Available from your Retailer

'Thread Painting' is the registered trademark of Gütermann & Co.
A.G. Zürich and is used in this book with their permission, approval
and co-operation.

British Library Cataloguing in Publication Data

Hubbard, Liz
   Thread painting.
   1. Embroidery, Machine
   I. Title
   746.44'028   TS1783

   ISBN 0–7153–9000–7

Typeset by ABM Typographics Limited, Hull
and printed in West Germany
by Mohndruck GmbH
for David & Charles Publishers plc
Brunel House   Newton Abbot   Devon

Distributed in the United States by
Sterling Publishing Co, Inc,
2 Park Avenue, New York, NY 10016